THE
DURHD

Long dist...
around the bou...

(Appro... ... ... miles)

Researched, compiled and Illustrated by
JILL DELANEY

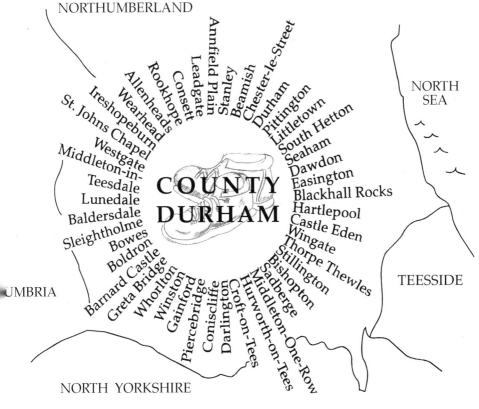

NORTHUMBERLAND

NORTH SEA

Annfield Plain
Leadgate
Consett
Rookhope
Allenheads
Wearhead
Ireshopeburn
St. Johns Chapel
Westgate
Middleton-in-Teesdale
Lunedale
Baldersdale
Sleightholme
Bowes
Boldron
Barnard Castle
Greta Bridge
Whorlton
Winston
Gainford
Piercebridge
Coniscliffe
Darlington
Croft-on-Tees
Hurworth-on-Tees
Middleton-One-Row
Sadberge
Bishopton
Stillington
Thorpe Thewles
Wingate
Castle Eden
Hartlepool
Blackhall Rocks
Easington
Dawdon
Seaham
South Hetton
Littletown
Pittington
Durham
Chester-le-Street
Beamish
Stanley

COUNTY DURHAM

UMBRIA

TEESSIDE

NORTH YORKSHIRE

A Challenge to Walkers

First Published by Printability Publishing Ltd., Wolviston. July 1997.
Designed and Printed by Atkinson Print Ltd., 11 Lower Church Street, Hartlepool, TS24 7DJ.
Tel: (01429) 267849   Fax: (01429) 865416
ISBN No. 1 872239 17 X

For John
– who gave me the idea –
and who led me on many walks
off the beaten track.

– and with thanks to all
those kind people who helped me
on my way –
particularly staff at the
Environment Department
County Hall, Durham
and my patient publisher
Brian Liddell.

HIGH FORCE
England's largest waterfall
– a dramatic drop over Great Whin Sill

CONTENTS

INTRODUCTION

The **Durham Round** is a county boundary trail for walkers around County Durham. It is a long-distance walk of some **155 miles (248 kilometres).** I think its diversity and infinite variety makes it possibly the most exciting circumambulation in Great Britain. There are great rivers, historic castles and abbeys, heroic waterfalls, industrial museums, sea ports, lead and coal mines, Roman remains, natural wilderness, and the highest public house in England.

A walker on the **Durham Round** will find that the route includes well-known paths such as parts of the Pennine Way. It uses parts of other long-distance walks such as —

> the Weardale Way
> the Wear Valley Way
> the Waskerley Way
> the Teesdale Way
> Haswell-Hart Walkway
> Castle Eden Walkway

and the Consett to Sunderland Railway Path. In addition there are five loops which leave the main route.

The Loops —

> The Hartlepool Loop – a chance to see historic ships in the process of restoration.
>
> The Barnard Castle Loop – for the Bowes Museum and Egglestone Abbey.
>
> Killhope Lead Mining Centre Loop.
>
> The Tan Hill Loop – As from 1991, the highest pub in England is now in Yorkshire but it is too close to the border to miss out.
>
> The Darlington Loop – for steam railway enthusiasts.

Whether or not to include any of these loops is a matter of personal choice, of course. The decision will most likely be made during your walk, with the weather and your own physical condition playing no small part.

The Middleton-in-Teesdale route is an alternative to the main route in case of poor visibility or should an easier walk along the Tees be desired. This is the safer route of the two.

The Route

The *Durham Round* does not always keep close to the county boundary and oocasionally leaves County Durham altogether, for example at Thorpe Thewles at the southern end of the Castle Eden Walkway. It crosses the River Tees at Croft-on-Tees into Yorkshire because there is a suitable path South of the river.

There are now more than five hundred miles of dismantled railways in County Durham which have been converted to foot and cycle paths by Durham County Council. The Waskerley Way, the Haswell-Hart Walkway and the Castle Eden Walkway were once railways used in the mining industries. The Consett to Sunderland Railway cycle path which was converted by Sustrans now has many site specific sculptures along its way, made from the remains of the industries which once supported the economy of the area. These paths are easier to walk and are more resistant to erosion than the arduous Durham Fells.

I have included many towns, villages and hamlets on the walk instead of bypassing them – in order to appreciate everything, the eye needs variety I think.

Points of Departure

I have chosen Durham City* as the starting point for the route maps because I think that it will probably be the most popular venue, especially for those not familiar with the county. It has the advantage of being fairly close to the county boundary, but then so are other towns such as Chester-le-Street*, Darlington*, Hartlepool* and Barnard Castle. The choice is yours – you could even start from Tan Hill and finish in Bowes or Barnard Castle. (*on B.R. railway stations)

Clockwise or anti-clockwise?

There is a good case for travelling clockwise if you plan to start in Durham City. This is because the Eastern part of the county is generally easier going than the treks across the Durham Fells in the West. The East is less isolated and more suitable to the early stages of the journey enabling the walker to adjust to the life-style more readily. The climate is dryer than on the Fells. Alternatively some walkers might prefer going anti-clockwise in order to cover the harder part of the walk during early days when they are at their freshest. If your starting point is in the more Southerly regions I advise going anti-clockwise following the Greta or the River Tees. It is not quite so easy to get lost when you are following a river, as it is when you are crossing the Fells on a misty day. Try to arrange your walk so that by the time you reach the more isolated regions you have become more acclimatised and 'path-wise'.

It is not possible to record and update all the changes which might take place between the time of writing and the moment you use this book to walk the *Durham Round.* This is one of the reasons for the need to take the following **Ordnance Survey Maps in the Landranger series.**

Number 92	–	Barnard Castle and surrounding area.
Number 93	–	Middlesbrough and Darlington area.
Number 87	–	Hexham, Haltwhistle and surrounding area.
Number 88	–	Tyneside and Durham.

You could also treat yourself to the Ordnance Survey Outdoor Leisure Map series 31 of Teesdale. It is a superb double sided one in the scale of 2.5 inches to the mile.

How long will it take to walk the *Durham Round?*

About two weeks should be allowed – (unless you want to break records) – this allows for about 11 miles a day – with plenty of time off – to visit places of interest.

The numerical system used will guide you from one map to the next. **Numbers found inset in an ellipse at the bottom left and top right of each page indicate the next page to turn to.**

Example:

MAP 50 – To Waskerley

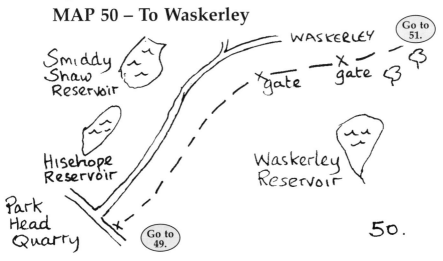

Occasionally, features at the end of one map, are repeated on the next to make map reading easier. Grid North is marked on each page and to read the route correctly you will have to turn the book until the printed arrow is pointing North.

Direction Finding

You will need a compass and some experience of using it. If you have not used one before, you will be an 'old hand' by the end of the walk – but give yourself some practice before you start. You will often have a back-up system – the sun. At midday turn your back on the sun and you will be facing North.

KEY TO SYMBOLS

— — Walker's route   - - - Other paths

G anti-clockwise walkers

☏ Telephone   F. B Footbridge

▲ Campsite

/ Stile   NORTH ← Grid North

✗ gate

- - - - railway path   +—+—+—+ railway

°° beach   ▲ trig point

▭▭▭ wall   ◌◌◌◌ hedge

🌳🌲🌳 trees   ⧄⧄⧄ crags

～～～ river or beck   ⌃⌃⌃ water/sea

Scale varies — for mileage on each map refer to Index to Maps on page 58.

MAP 1 – Durham City

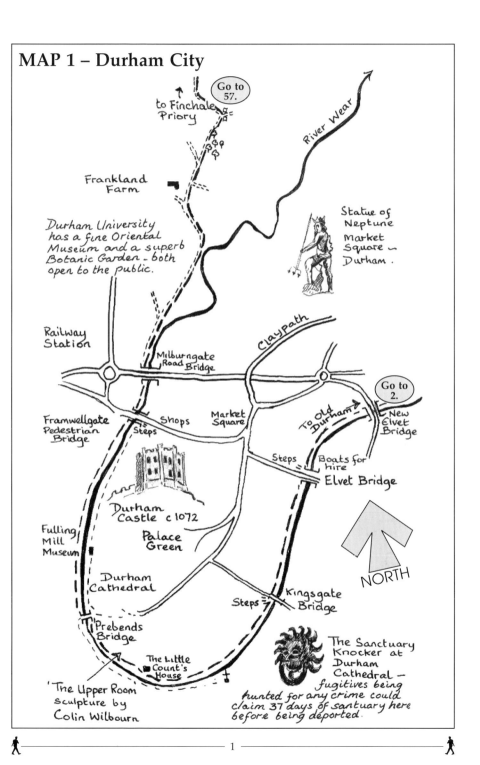

to Finchale Priory

Go to 57.

River Wear

Frankland Farm

Durham University has a fine Oriental Museum and a superb Botanic Garden – both open to the public.

Statue of Neptune Market Square – Durham.

Railway Station

Claypath

Milburngate Road Bridge

Go to 2.

Framwellgate Pedestrian Bridge

Shops
Steps

Market Square

To Old Durham

New Elvet Bridge

Steps

Boats for hire

Elvet Bridge

Durham Castle c 1072

Palace Green

NORTH

Fulling Mill Museum

Durham Cathedral

Steps

Kingsgate Bridge

Prebends Bridge

The Little Count's House

'The Upper Room' sculpture by Colin Wilbourn

The Sanctuary Knocker at Durham Cathedral – fugitives being hunted for any crime could claim 37 days of sanctuary here before being deported.

MAP 2 – Old Durham

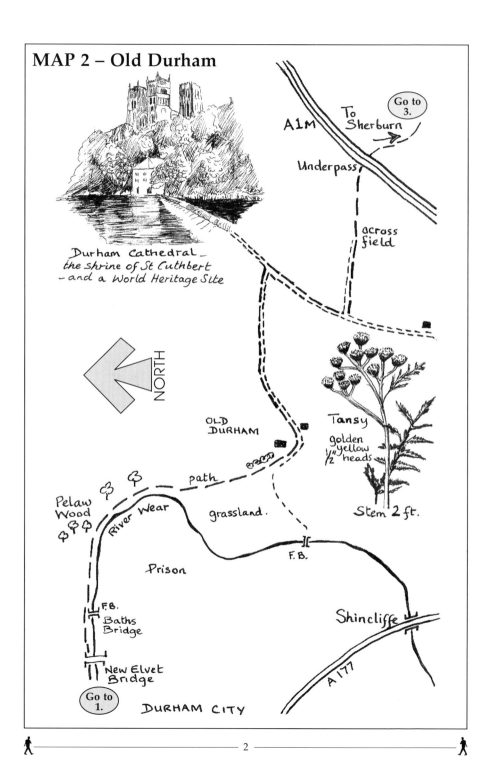

Durham Cathedral
the shrine of St Cuthbert
– and a World Heritage Site

A1M

To Sherburn

Go to 3.

Underpass

across field

NORTH

OLD DURHAM

Tansy
golden ½" yellow heads

Stem 2 ft.

path

Pelaw Wood

River Wear

grassland

F.B.

Prison

F.B.
Baths Bridge

Shincliffe

A 177

New Elvet Bridge

Go to 1.

DURHAM CITY

MAP 3 – Sherburn – Low Pittington

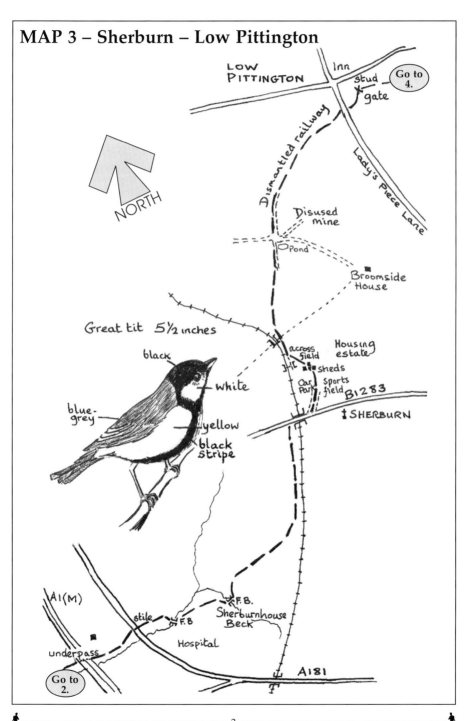

LOW PITTINGTON

Inn

Go to 4.

stud gate

Lady's Piece Lane

Dismantled railway

Disused mine

Pond

Broomside House

Great tit 5½ inches

black

white

blue-grey

yellow

black stripe

across field

Housing estate

sheds

Car Park

Sports field

B1283

✝ SHERBURN

A1(M)

stile

F.B

F.B. Sherburnhouse Beck

Hospital

underpass

Go to 2.

A181

MAP 4 – To Littletown

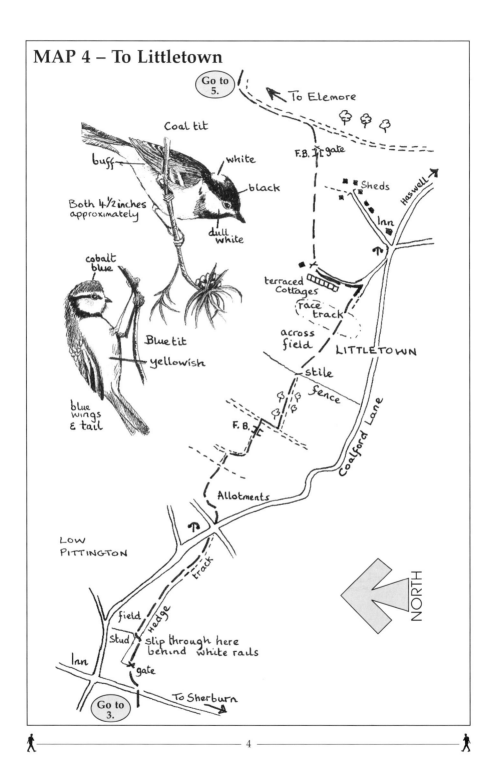

Go to 5.

To Elemore

Coal tit

white

black

buff

dull white

Both 4½ inches approximately

F.B. & gate

Sheds

Haswell

Inn

terraced Cottages

race track

across field

LITTLETOWN

cobalt blue

Blue tit

yellowish

stile

fence

blue wings & tail

F. B.

Coalford Lane

Allotments

LOW PITTINGTON

track

NORTH

field

hedge

Stud

slip through here behind white rails

Inn

gate

Go to 3.

To Sherburn

4

MAP 5 – To South Hetton

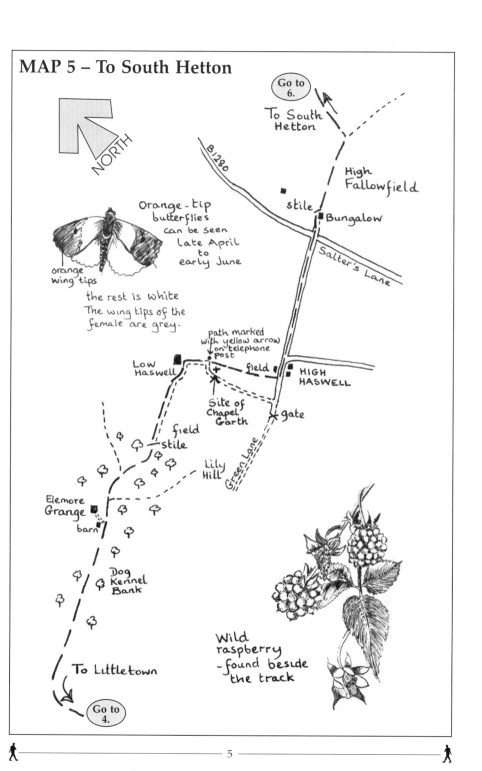

NORTH

Go to 6.

To South Hetton

B1280

High Fallowfield

stile

Bungalow

Salter's Lane

Orange-tip butterflies can be seen late April to early June

orange wing tips

the rest is white
The wing tips of the female are grey.

path marked with yellow arrow on telephone post

Low Haswell

field

HIGH HASWELL

Site of Chapel Garth

gate

field stile

Lily Hill

Green Lane

Elemore Grange

barn

Dog Kennel Bank

To Littletown

Wild raspberry – found beside the track

Go to 4.

MAP 6 – To Seaham

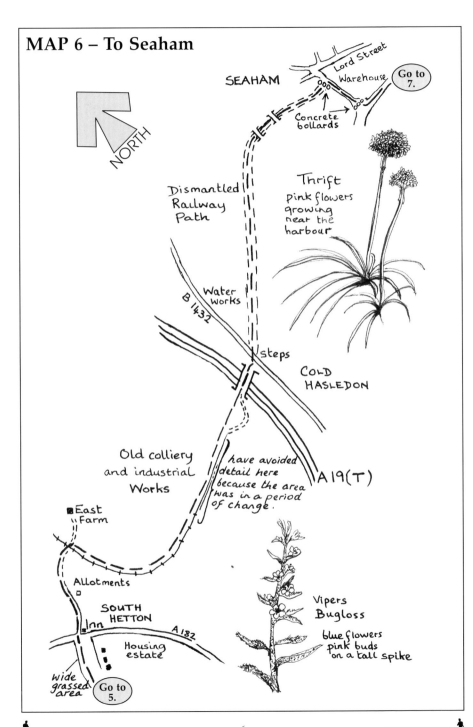

SEAHAM

Lord Street

Warehouse

Go to 7.

Concrete bollards

NORTH

Dismantled Railway Path

Thrift
pink flowers growing near the harbour

Water works

B 1432

steps

COLD HASLEDON

Old colliery and industrial Works

have avoided detail here because the area was in a period of change.

A19(T)

East Farm

Allotments

Vipers Bugloss

blue flowers pink buds on a tall spike

SOUTH HETTON

Inn

A182

Housing estate

wide grassed area

Go to 5.

MAP 7 – To Blast Beach

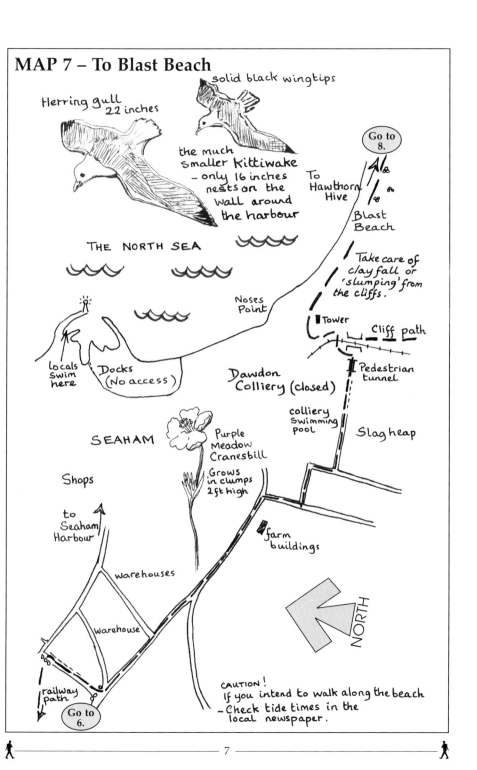

Herring gull
22 inches

solid black wingtips

the much
smaller Kittiwake
– only 16 inches
nests on the
wall around
the harbour

To
Hawthorn
Hive

Go to
8.

Blast
Beach

THE NORTH SEA

Take care of
clay fall or
'slumping' from
the cliffs.

Noses
Point

Tower

Cliff path

locals
Swim
here

Docks
(No access)

Dawdon
Colliery (closed)

Pedestrian
tunnel

colliery
swimming
pool

Slag heap

SEAHAM

Purple
Meadow
Cranesbill

Shops

Grows
in clumps
2ft high

to
Seaham
Harbour

farm
buildings

warehouses

NORTH

warehouse

railway
path

Go to
6.

CAUTION!
If you intend to walk along the beach
– Check tide times in the
local newspaper.

MAP 8 – To Foxholes

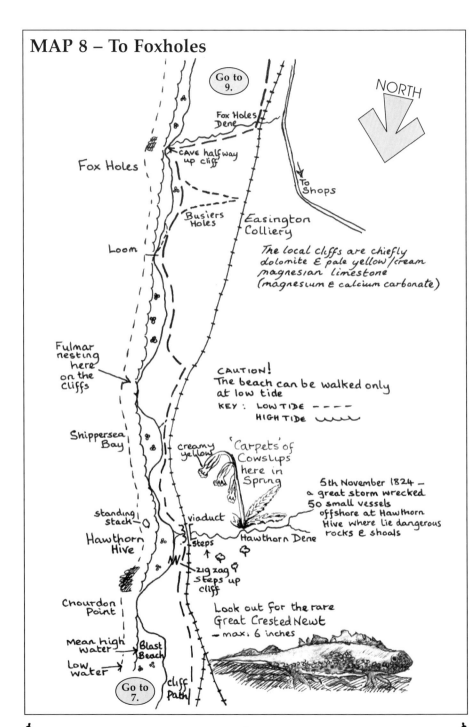

Go to 9.

NORTH

Fox Holes Dene

CAVE half way up cliff

Fox Holes

To Shops

Busiers Holes

Easington Colliery

Loom

The local cliffs are chiefly dolomite & pale yellow/cream magnesian limestone (magnesium & calcium carbonate)

Fulmar nesting here on the cliffs

CAUTION!
The beach can be walked only at low tide
KEY: LOW TIDE – – – –
HIGH TIDE 〰〰〰

Shippersea Bay

creamy yellow

'Carpets' of Cowslips here in Spring

5th November 1824 – a great storm wrecked 50 small vessels offshore at Hawthorn Hive where lie dangerous rocks & shoals

standing stack

viaduct

Hawthorn Hive

steps

Hawthorn Dene

zig zag steps up cliff

Chourdon Point

Look out for the rare Great Crested Newt – max. 6 inches

Mean high water

Blast Beach

Low water

Go to 7.

cliff path

8

MAP 9 – To Blackhall Rocks

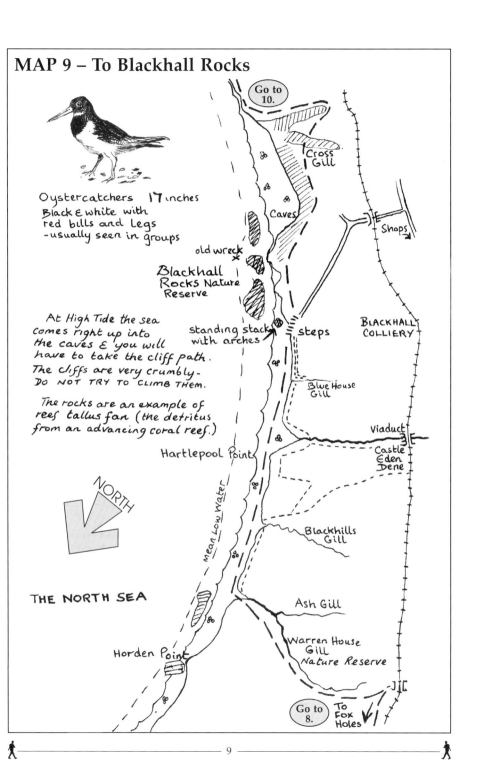

Go to 10.

Oystercatchers 17 inches
Black & white with
red bills and legs
-usually seen in groups

Cross Gill

Caves

old wreck ✗

Blackhall Rocks Nature Reserve

Shops

At High Tide the sea comes right up into the caves & you will have to take the cliff path. The cliffs are very crumbly - DO NOT TRY TO CLIMB THEM.

The rocks are an example of reef tallus fan (the detritus from an advancing coral reef.)

standing stack with arches

steps

BLACKHALL COLLIERY

Blue House Gill

Hartlepool Point

Viaduct

Castle Eden Dene

NORTH

Mean Low Water

THE NORTH SEA

Blackhills Gill

Ash Gill

Horden Point

Warren House Gill Nature Reserve

Go to 8.

To Fox Holes

9

MAP 10 – To Crimdon

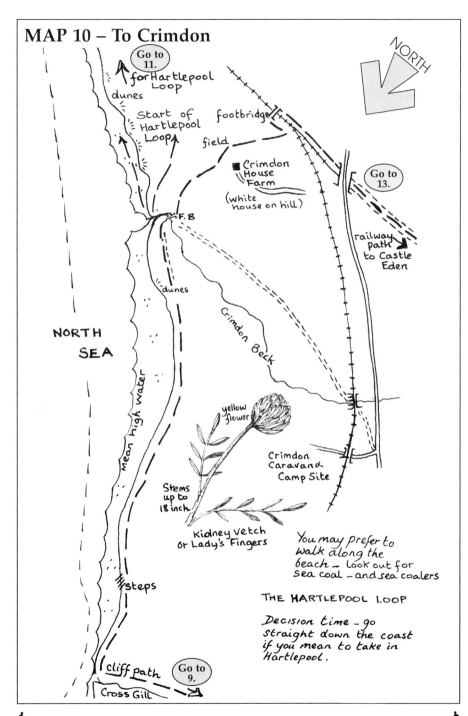

NORTH

Go to 11.

↑ for Hartlepool Loop

dunes

Start of Hartlepool Loop ↑

footbridge

field

■ Crimdon House Farm

(white house on hill)

Go to 13.

F.B

railway path to Castle Eden

dunes

Crimdon Beck

NORTH SEA

Mean high water

yellow flower

Crimdon Caravand Camp Site

Stems up to 18 inch

Kidney vetch or Lady's Fingers

You may prefer to walk along the beach — look out for sea coal — and sea coalers

THE HARTLEPOOL LOOP

Decision time — go straight down the coast if you mean to take in Hartlepool.

steps

cliff path

Go to 9.

Cross Gill

MAP 11 – To Hartlepool

The Hartlepool Loop

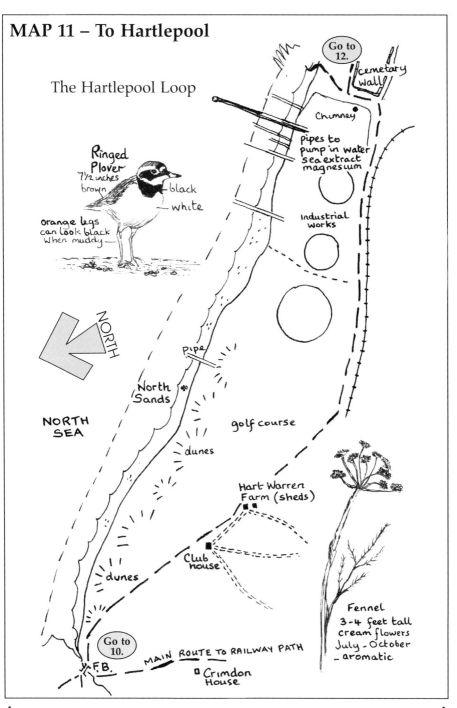

Go to
12.

cemetery
wall

Chimney

pipes to
pump in water
sea extract
magnesium

Industrial
works

Ringed
Plover
7½ inches
brown
— black
— white

orange legs
can look black
when muddy —

NORTH

Pipe

North
Sands

NORTH
SEA

golf course

dunes

Hart Warren
Farm (sheds)

Club
house

dunes

Go to
10.

F.B.

MAIN ROUTE TO RAILWAY PATH

Crimdon
House

Fennel
3–4 feet tall
cream flowers
July – October
– aromatic

MAP 12 – *The Hartlepool Loop*

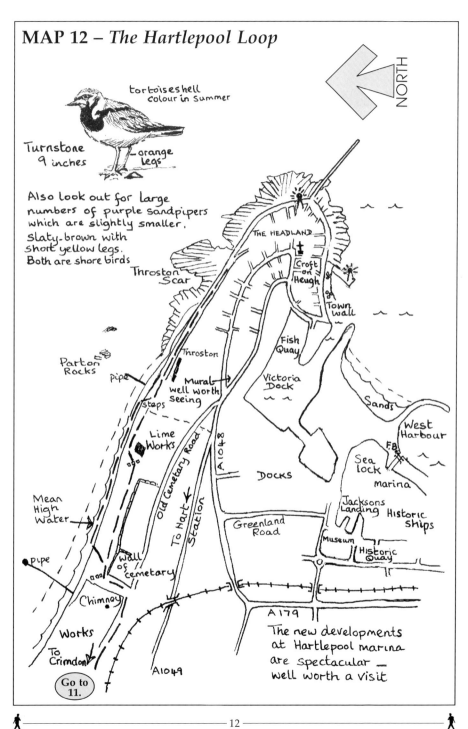

NORTH

tortoiseshell colour in Summer

Turnstone 9 inches

orange legs

Also look out for large numbers of purple sandpipers which are slightly smaller.
Slaty-brown with short yellow legs.
Both are shore birds

THE HEADLAND

Throston Scar

Croft on Heugh

Town wall

Parton Rocks

Throston

Fish Quay

pipe

Mural well worth seeing

Victoria Dock

Sands

staps

West Harbour

Lime Works

Old Cemetary Road

A 178

FB

Sea lock

marina

Docks

Mean High Water

To Hart Station

Jacksons Landing

Historic Ships

Greenland Road

Museum

Historic Quay

pipe

Wall of cemetary

Chimney

A179

Works

To Crimdon

A1049

Go to 11.

The new developments at Hartlepool marina are spectacular – well worth a visit

MAP 13 – To Castle Eden

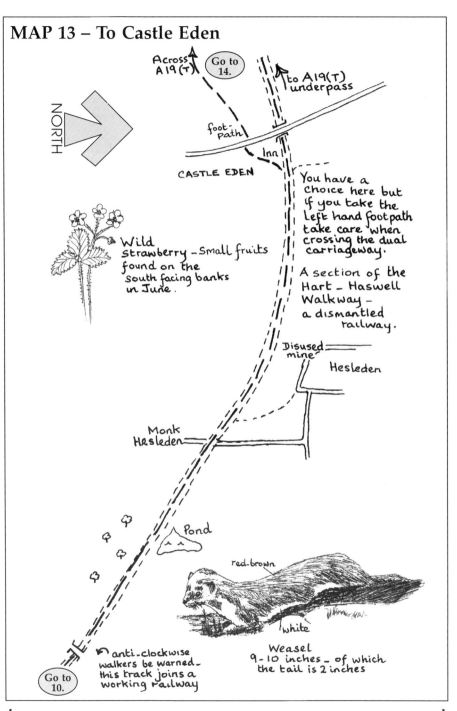

Across A19(T)

Go to 14.

to A19(T) underpass

foot-path

Inn

CASTLE EDEN

NORTH

You have a choice here but if you take the left hand footpath take care when crossing the dual carriageway.

Wild strawberry – Small fruits found on the south facing banks in June.

A section of the Hart – Haswell Walkway – a dismantled railway.

Disused mine

Hesleden

Monk Hesleden

Pond

red-brown

white

Weasel
9-10 inches – of which the tail is 2 inches

Go to 10.

anti-clockwise walkers be warned – this track joins a working railway

MAP 14 – To Wingate

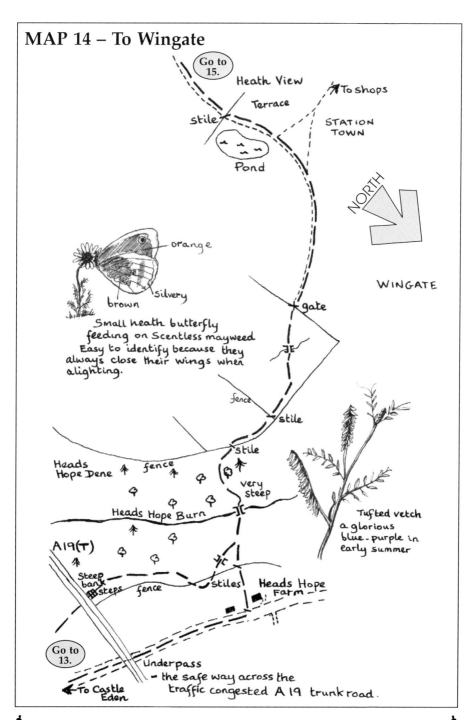

Go to 15.

Heath View

To shops

Terrace

STATION TOWN

stile

Pond

NORTH

WINGATE

orange

silvery

brown

Small heath butterfly feeding on Scentless mayweed Easy to identify because they always close their wings when alighting.

gate

fence

stile

stile

Heads Hope Dene

fence

very steep

Heads Hope Burn

Tufted vetch a glorious blue-purple in early summer

A19(T)

Steep bank steps

fence

stiles

Heads Hope Farm

Go to 13.

Underpass – the safe way across the traffic congested A 19 trunk road.

To Castle Eden

MAP 15 – Station Town

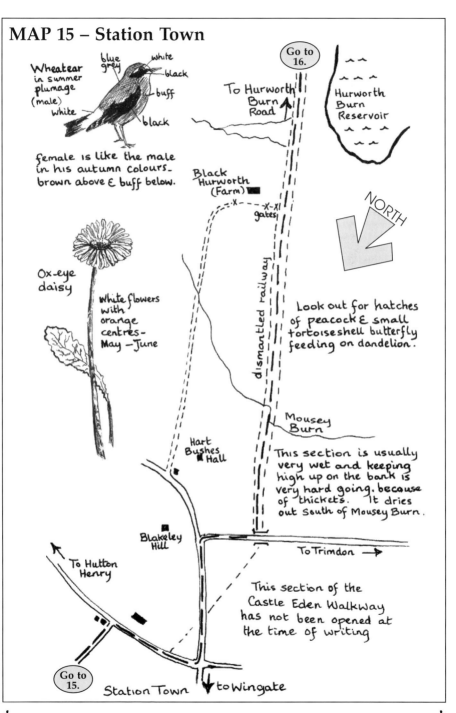

Wheatear in summer plumage (male)

blue grey
white
black
buff
white
black

female is like the male in his autumn colours. brown above & buff below.

Ox-eye daisy

White flowers with orange centres. May – June

Go to 16.

To Hurworth Burn Road

Hurworth Burn Reservoir

Black Hurworth (Farm)

gates

NORTH

dismantled railway

Look out for hatches of peacock & small tortoiseshell butterfly feeding on dandelion.

Mousey Burn

This section is usually very wet and keeping high up on the bank is very hard going. because of thickets. It dries out south of Mousey Burn.

Hart Bushes Hall

Blakeley Hill

To Trimdon →

To Hutton Henry

This section of the Castle Eden Walkway has not been opened at the time of writing

Go to 15.

Station Town

to Wingate

15

MAP 16 – Hurworth Burn

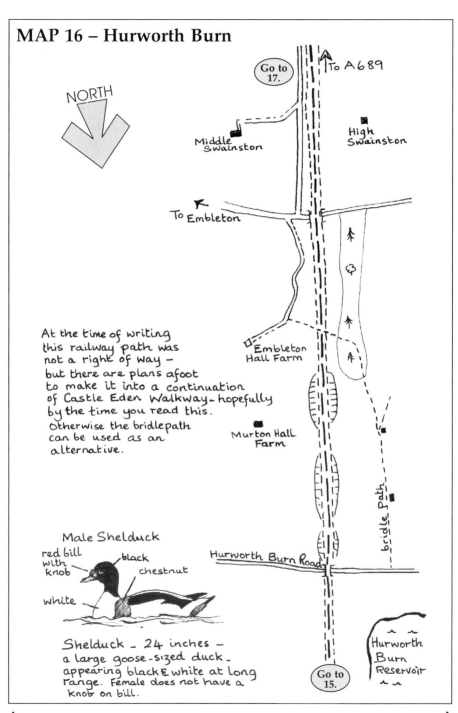

NORTH

Go to 17.

To A689

Middle Swainston

High Swainston

To Embleton

Embleton Hall Farm

At the time of writing this railway path was not a right of way — but there are plans afoot to make it into a continuation of Castle Eden Walkway - hopefully by the time you read this. Otherwise the bridlepath can be used as an alternative.

Murton Hall Farm

bridle path

Male Shelduck

red bill with knob

black

chestnut

white

Hurworth Burn Road

Go to 15.

Hurworth Burn Reservoir

Shelduck _ 24 inches _ a large goose-sized duck _ appearing black & white at long range. Female does not have a knob on bill.

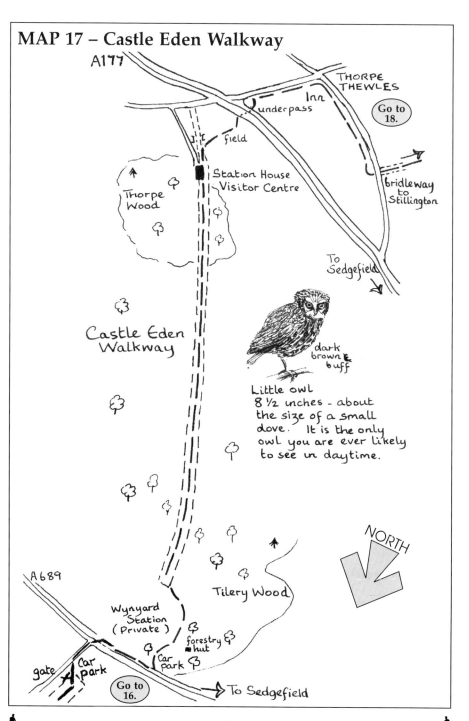

MAP 17 – Castle Eden Walkway

A177

THORPE THEWLES

Inn

underpass

Go to 18.

field

Station House Visitor Centre

bridleway to Stillington

Thorpe Wood

To Sedgefield

Castle Eden Walkway

dark brown buff

Little owl
8 ½ inches - about the size of a small dove. It is the only owl you are ever likely to see in daytime.

NORTH

A689

Tilery Wood

Wynyard Station (Private)

forestry hut

Car park

gate Car park

Go to 16.

To Sedgefield

17

MAP 18 – To Stillington

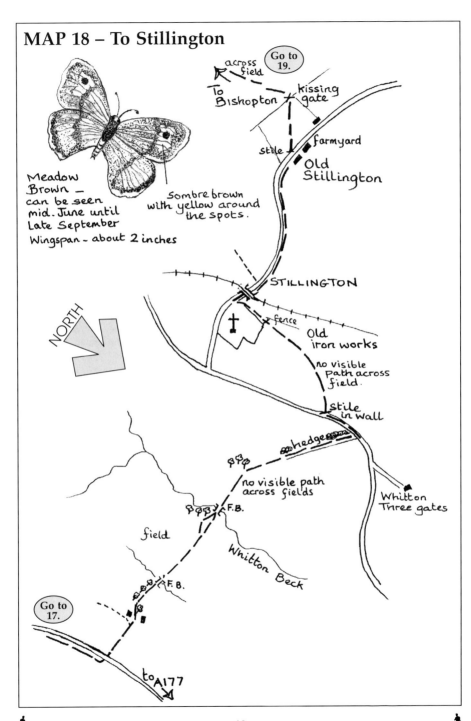

Go to 19.

across field

To Bishopton

kissing gate

stile

farmyard

Old Stillington

Meadow Brown – can be seen mid. June until Late September

Wingspan – about 2 inches

Sombre brown with yellow around the spots.

STILLINGTON

NORTH

fence

Old iron works

no visible path across field.

stile in wall

hedge

no visible path across fields

F.B.

Whitton Three gates

field

Whitton Beck

F.B.

Go to 17.

to A177

MAP 19 – Bishopton

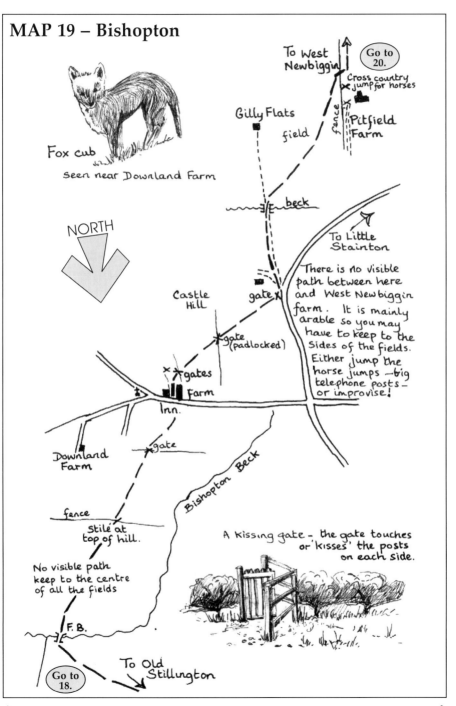

Fox cub

Seen near Downland Farm

NORTH

To West Newbiggin

Go to 20.

Cross country jump for horses

Gilly Flats

field

fence

Pitfield Farm

beck

To Little Stainton

There is no visible path between here and West Newbiggin farm. It is mainly arable so you may have to keep to the sides of the fields. Either jump the horse jumps – big telephone posts – or improvise!

Castle Hill

gate

gate (padlocked)

gates

Farm

Inn.

Downland Farm

gate

Bishopton Beck

fence

Stile at top of hill.

No visible path keep to the centre of all the fields

A kissing gate – the gate touches or 'kisses' the posts on each side.

F.B.

Go to 18.

To Old Stillington

19

MAP 20 – Sadberge

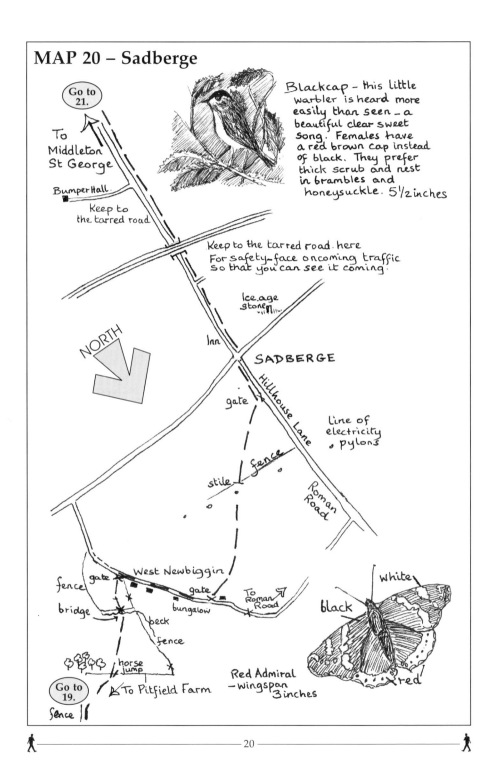

Go to 21.

To Middleton St George

Bumper Hall.

Keep to the tarred road

Keep to the tarred road. here
For safety face oncoming traffic
so that you can see it coming.

Blackcap – this little warbler is heard more easily than seen – a beautiful clear sweet song. Females have a red brown cap instead of black. They prefer thick scrub and nest in brambles and honeysuckle. 5½ inches

Ice age stone

Inn

NORTH

SADBERGE

gate

Hillhouse Lane

Line of electricity pylons

stile fence

Roman Road

fence gate West Newbiggin

bridge

beck

fence

gate

To Roman Road

bungalow

horse jump

Go to 19.

fence

To Pitfield Farm

Red Admiral –wingspan 3inches

white

black

red

MAP 21 – To Oak Tree

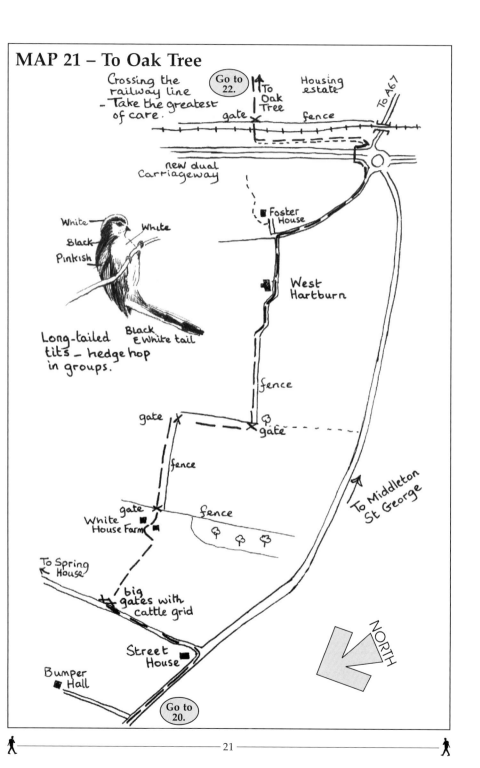

Crossing the railway line
- Take the greatest of care.

Go to 22.

To Oak Tree

Housing estate

To A67

gate

fence

new dual Carriageway

Foster House

West Hartburn

White

White

Black

Pinkish

Long-tailed tits – hedge hop in groups.

Black & White tail

fence

gate

gate

fence

To Middleton St George

gate

White House Farm

fence

To Spring House

big gates with cattle grid

NORTH

Street House

Bumper Hall

Go to 20.

MAP 22 – To Middleton-One-Row

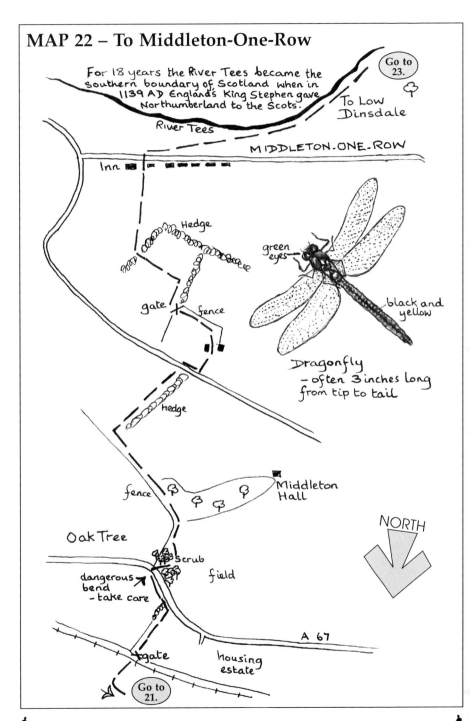

For 18 years the River Tees became the southern boundary of Scotland when in 1139 AD England's King Stephen gave Northumberland to the Scots.

River Tees

Go to 23.

To Low Dinsdale

MIDDLETON-ONE-ROW

Inn

Hedge

green eyes

gate

fence

black and yellow

Dragonfly
– often 3 inches long from tip to tail

hedge

fence

Middleton Hall

NORTH

Oak Tree

dangerous bend – take care

Scrub

field

A 67

gate

housing estate

Go to 21.

MAP 23 – Dinsdale to Girsby

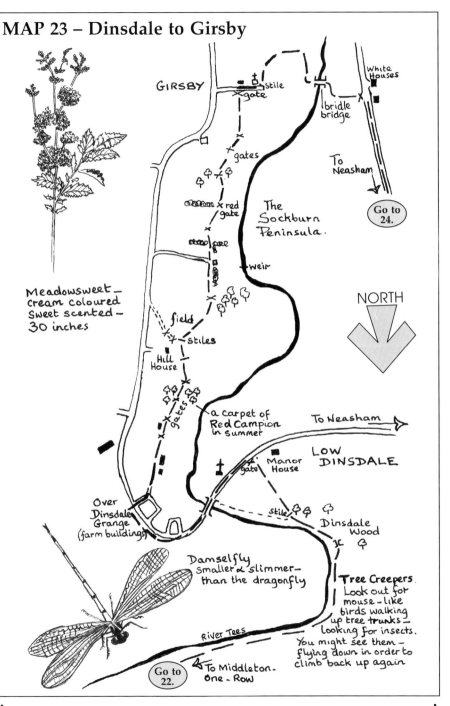

GIRSBY

stile
gate

White Houses

bridle
bridge

To Neasham

gates

red gate

Go to 24.

The Sockburn Peninsula.

weir

Meadowsweet —
cream coloured
sweet scented —
30 inches

field

stiles

Hill House

NORTH

gates

a carpet of Red Campion in summer

To Neasham

LOW DINSDALE

Manor House

gate

Over Dinsdale Grange (farm buildings)

stile

Dinsdale Wood

Damselfly
smaller & slimmer —
than the dragonfly

Tree Creepers.
Look out for
mouse-like
birds walking
up tree trunks —
looking for insects.
You might see them —
flying down in order to
climb back up again

River Tees

Go to 22.

To Middleton-
One-Row

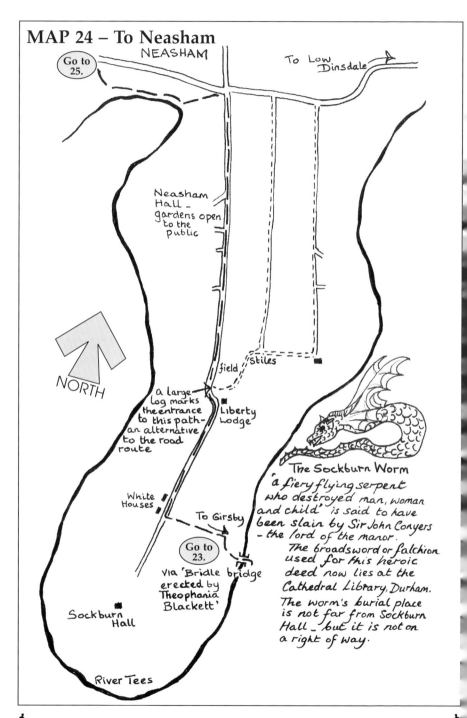

MAP 24 – To Neasham

NEASHAM

To Low Dinsdale

Go to 25.

Neasham Hall – gardens open to the public

NORTH

field stiles

a large log marks the entrance to this path – an alternative to the road route

Liberty Lodge

The Sockburn Worm 'a fiery flying serpent who destroyed man, woman and child' is said to have been slain by Sir John Conyers – the lord of the manor.

The broadsword or falchion used for this heroic deed now lies at the Cathedral Library, Durham.

White Houses

To Girsby

Go to 23.

via 'Bridle bridge erected by Theophania Blackett'

The worm's burial place is not far from Sockburn Hall – but it is not on a right of way.

Sockburn Hall

River Tees

MAP 25 – Hurworth and Croft – on-Tees

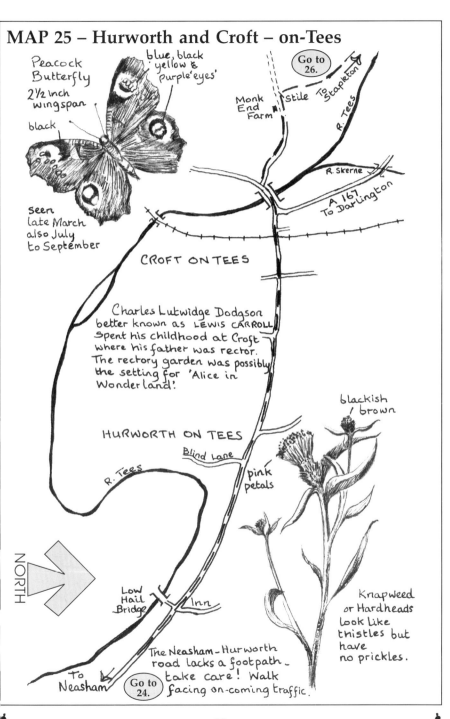

Peacock Butterfly

2½ inch wingspan

blue, black yellow & purple 'eyes'

black

Seen late March also July to September

Go to 26.

Monk End Farm

Stile To Stapleton

R. Tees

R. Skerne

A 167 To Darlington

CROFT ON TEES

Charles Lutwidge Dodgson better known as LEWIS CARROLL spent his childhood at Croft where his father was rector. The rectory garden was possibly the setting for 'Alice in Wonderland'.

HURWORTH ON TEES

Blind Lane

R. Tees

pink petals

blackish / brown

NORTH

Low Hail Bridge

Inn

Knapweed or Hardheads look like thistles but have no prickles.

To Neasham

Go to 24.

The Neasham-Hurworth road lacks a footpath – take care! Walk facing on-coming traffic.

MAP 26 – To Blackwell

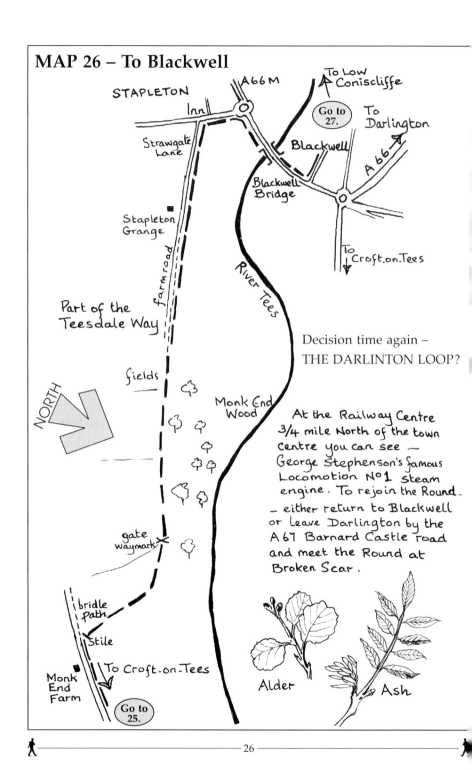

STAPLETON

A66M

To Low Coniscliffe

Inn

Go to 27.

To Darlington

A66

Strawgate Lane

Blackwell

Stapleton Grange

Blackwell Bridge

farm road

To Croft-on-Tees

River Tees

Part of the Teesdale Way

Decision time again –
THE DARLINTON LOOP?

fields

NORTH

Monk End Wood

At the Railway Centre 3/4 mile North of the town centre you can see – George Stephenson's famous Locomotion Nº1 steam engine. To rejoin the Round – either return to Blackwell or leave Darlington by the A67 Barnard Castle road and meet the Round at Broken Scar.

gate waymark

bridle path

Stile

Monk End Farm

To Croft-on-Tees

Alder

Ash

Go to 25.

MAP 27 – Low Coniscliffe

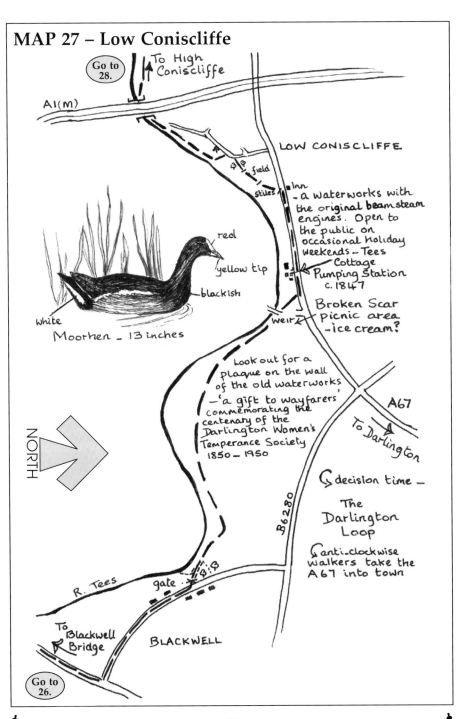

Go to 28.

To High Coniscliffe

A1(m)

LOW CONISCLIFFE

field

stiles

Inn

- a waterworks with the original beam steam engines. Open to the public on occasional holiday weekends – Tees Cottage Pumping Station c. 1847

red

yellow tip

blackish

white

Moorhen – 13 inches

weir

Broken Scar picnic area – ice cream?

Look out for a plaque on the wall of the old waterworks – 'a gift to wayfarers' commemorating the centenary of the Darlington Women's Temperance Society 1850 – 1950

NORTH

A67

To Darlington

B6280

decision time –

The Darlington Loop

anti-clockwise walkers take the A67 into town

R. Tees

gate

To Blackwell Bridge

BLACKWELL

Go to 26.

MAP 28 – To Piercebridge

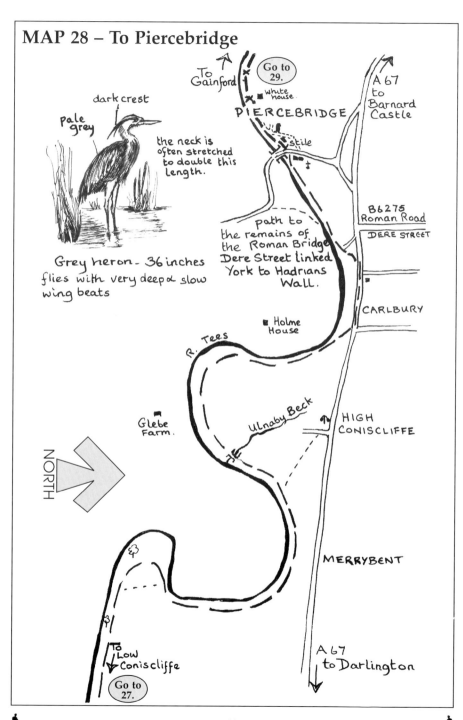

To Gainford

Go to 29.

white house

A 67 to Barnard Castle

PIERCEBRIDGE

stile

dark crest

pale grey

the neck is often stretched to double this length.

Grey heron - 36 inches flies with very deep & slow wing beats

B6275 Roman Road

DERE STREET

path to the remains of the Roman Bridge Dere Street linked York to Hadrians Wall.

CARLBURY

Holme House

R. Tees

NORTH

Glebe Farm.

Ulnaby Beck

HIGH CONISCLIFFE

MERRYBENT

To Low Coniscliffe

Go to 27.

A 67 to Darlington

MAP 29 – Gainford

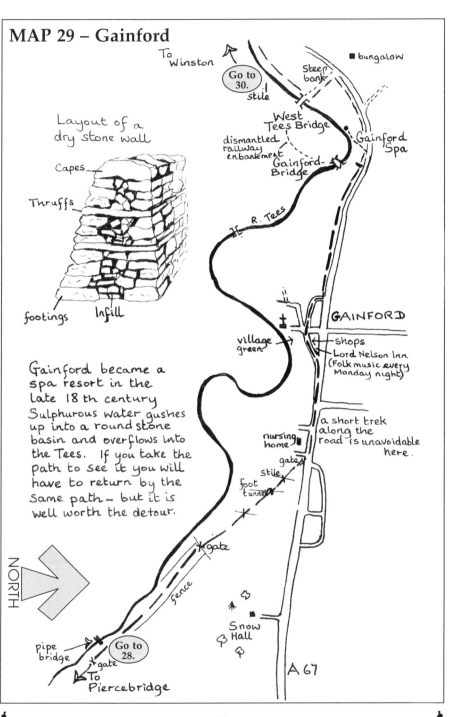

To Winston

■ bungalow

Go to 30.

stile

steep bank

West Tees Bridge

dismantled railway enbankment

Gainford-Bridge

Gainford Spa

Layout of a dry stone wall

Capes

Thruffs

R. Tees

footings   Infill

GAINFORD

village green

shops
Lord Nelson Inn
(Folk music every Monday night)

Gainford became a spa resort in the late 18th century Sulphurous water gushes up into a round stone basin and overflows into the Tees. If you take the path to see it you will have to return by the same path – but it is well worth the detour.

a short trek along the road is unavoidable here.

nursing home

gate

stile

foot tunnel

NORTH

gate

fence

Snow Hall

pipe bridge

Go to 28.

gate

To Piercebridge

A 67

MAP 30 – Winston – Whorlton

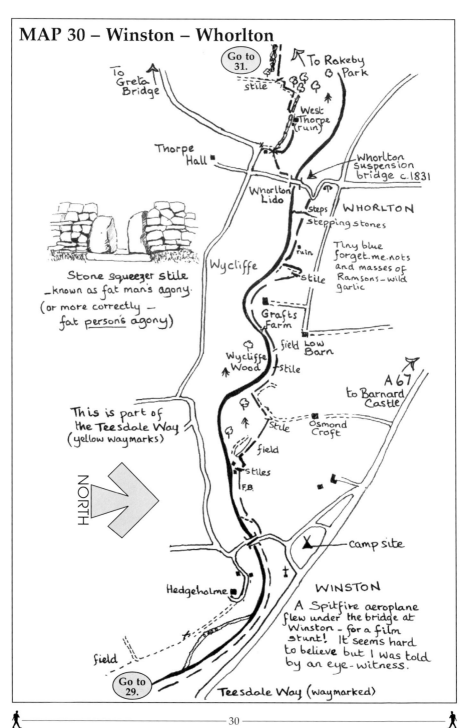

To Greta Bridge

Go to 31.

To Rokeby Park

stile

West Thorpe (ruin)

Thorpe Hall

Whorlton Suspension bridge c.1831

Whorlton Lido

steps WHORLTON

stepping stones

ruin

Tiny blue forget.me.nots and masses of Ramsons - wild garlic

Wycliffe

stile

Stone squeezer stile
_known as fat man's agony.
(or more correctly _
fat person's agony)

Grafts Farm

field Low Barn

Wycliffe Wood

stile

A 67
to Barnard Castle

This is part of
the Teesdale Way
(yellow waymarks)

stile Osmond Croft

field

NORTH

stiles

F.B.

camp site

Hedgeholme

WINSTON

A Spitfire aeroplane
flew under the bridge at
Winston - for a film
stunt! It seems hard
to believe but I was told
by an eye-witness.

field

Go to 29.

Teesdale Way (waymarked)

30

MAP 31 – Greta Bridge

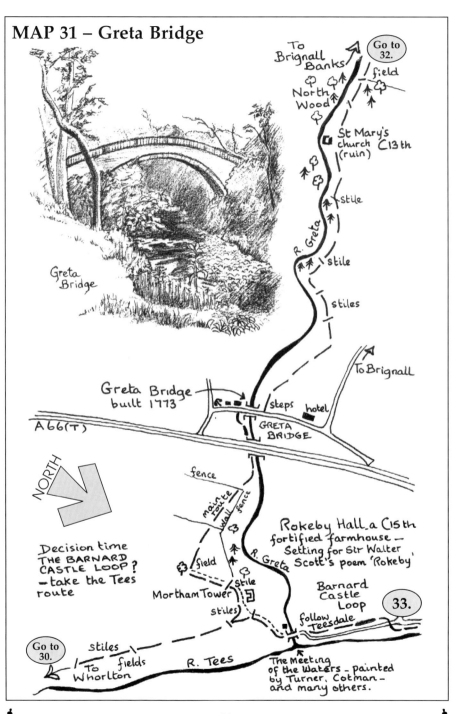

To Brignall Banks

Go to 32.

field

North Wood

St Mary's church (ruin) C13th

stile

R. Greta

stile

stiles

To Brignall

Greta Bridge built 1773

steps   hotel

GRETA BRIDGE

A 66 (T)

NORTH

main route   wall   fence

fence

Rokeby Hall a C15th fortified farmhouse – Setting for Sir Walter Scott's poem 'Rokeby'

Decision time THE BARNARD CASTLE LOOP? – take the Tees route

field

R. Greta

stile

Mortham Tower

stiles

Barnard Castle Loop

33.

follow Teesdale

Go to 30.

stiles   To fields Whorlton

R. Tees

The Meeting of the Waters – painted by Turner, Cotman – and many others.

Greta Bridge

31

MAP 32 – Brignall Banks

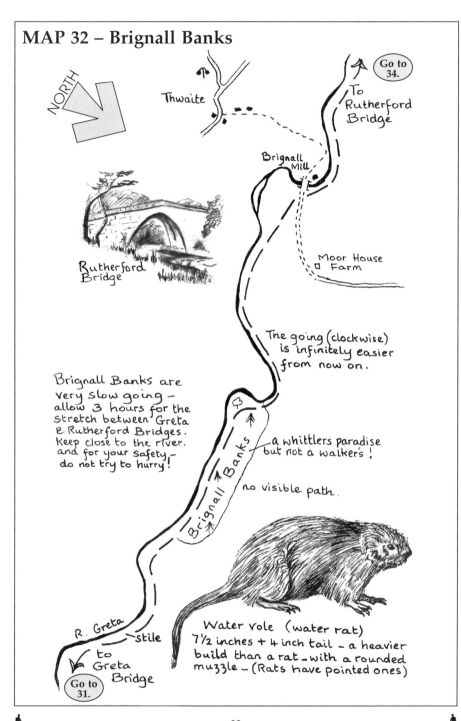

NORTH

Thwaite

Go to 34.

To Rutherford Bridge

Brignall Mill

Rutherford Bridge

Moor House Farm

The going (clockwise) is infinitely easier from now on.

Brignall Banks are very slow going – allow 3 hours for the stretch between Greta & Rutherford Bridges. Keep close to the river. and for your safety – do not try to hurry!

Brignall Banks

a whittlers paradise but not a walker's !

no visible path.

R. Greta

stile

to Greta Bridge

Go to 31.

Water vole (water rat) 7½ inches + 4 inch tail – a heavier build than a rat – with a rounded muzzle – (Rats have pointed ones)

MAP 33 – *The Barnard Castle Loop*

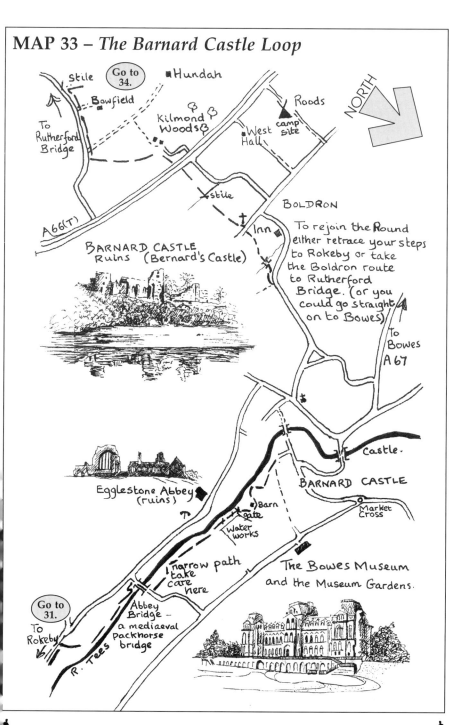

Stile

Go to 34.

■Hundah

····Bowfield

To
Rutherford
Bridge

Kilmond
Woods

Roods

West
Hall

camp
site

NORTH

stile

A66(T)

BOLDRON

Inn

BARNARD CASTLE
Ruins   (Bernard's Castle)

To rejoin the Round
either retrace your steps
to Rokeby or take
the Boldron route
to Rutherford
Bridge. (or you
could go straight
on to Bowes)

To
Bowes
A67

Egglestone Abbey
(ruins)

Barn
gate

Water
works

narrow path
take
care
here

Castle.

BARNARD CASTLE

Market
Cross

The Bowes Museum
and the Museum Gardens.

Go to
31.

To
Rokeby

Abbey
Bridge –
a mediaeval
packhorse
bridge

R. Tees

MAP 34 – To Gilmonby

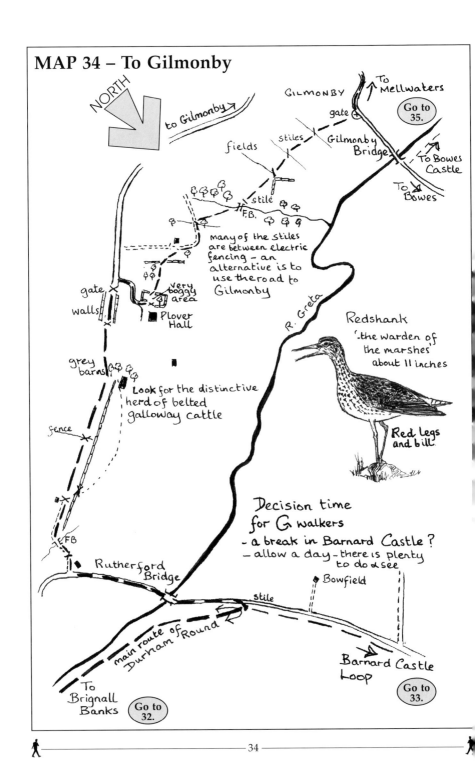

NORTH

to Gilmonby →

GILMONBY

To Mellwaters ↗

gate ⊕

Go to 35.

stiles

Gilmonby Bridge

↗ To Bowes Castle

fields

To Bowes

stile

F.B.

many of the stiles are between electric fencing – an alternative is to use the road to Gilmonby

gate ✕

walls

very boggy area

Plover Hall

R. Greta

Redshank

'the warden of the marshes' about 11 inches

grey barns

Look for the distinctive herd of belted galloway cattle

fence

Red legs and bill.

FB

Rutherford Bridge

Decision time for G walkers
- a break in Barnard Castle?
- allow a day – there is plenty to do & see

Bowfield

stile

main route of Durham Round

Barnard Castle Loop

Go to 33.

To Brignall Banks

Go to 32.

MAP 35 – To Mellwaters

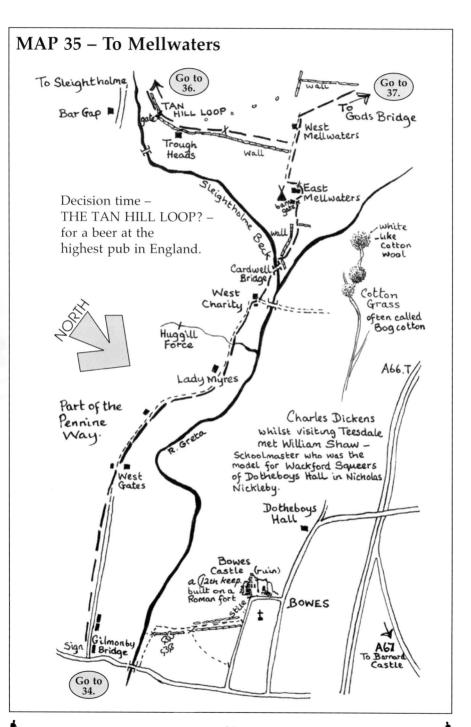

To Sleightholme,

Bar Gap

Go to 36.

Go to 37.

TAN HILL LOOP

wall

West Mellwaters

To Gods Bridge

Trough Heads

wall

Sleightholme Beck

Decision time –
THE TAN HILL LOOP? –
for a beer at the
highest pub in England.

East Mellwaters

barn gate

wall

white -like cotton wool

Cardwell Bridge

West Charity

Cotton Grass
often called Bog cotton

NORTH

Huggill Force

A66.T

Lady Myres

Part of the Pennine Way.

R. Greta

Charles Dickens
whilst visiting Teesdale
met William Shaw –
Schoolmaster who was the
model for Wackford Squeers
of Dotheboys Hall in Nicholas
Nickleby.

West Gates

Dotheboys Hall

Bowes Castle (ruin)
a 12th keep
built on a
Roman fort

stile

BOWES

Sign

Gilmonby Bridge

A67
To Barnard Castle

Go to 34.

35

MAP 36 – *Tan Hill Loop*

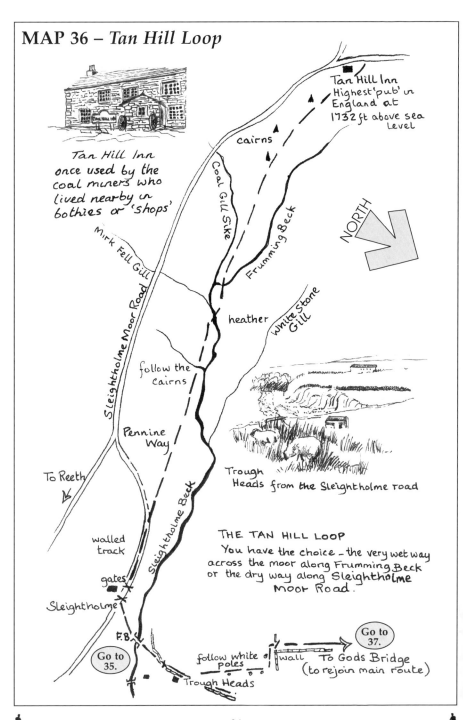

Tan Hill Inn
Highest 'pub' in
England at
1732 ft above sea
Level

cairns

Tan Hill Inn
once used by the
coal miners who
lived nearby in
bothies or 'shops'

Coal Gill Sike

Frumming Beck

NORTH

Mirk Fell Gill

Sleightholme Moor Road

heather

White Stone Gill

follow the
cairns

Pennine
Way

To Reeth

Sleightholme Beck

Trough
Heads from the Sleightholme road

THE TAN HILL LOOP

You have the choice – the very wet way
across the moor along Frumming Beck
or the dry way along Sleightholme
Moor Road.

walled
track

gates

Sleightholme

F.B.

Go to
35.

Go to
37.

follow white
poles

wall

To Gods Bridge
(to rejoin main route)

Trough Heads

MAP 37 – To Baldersdale

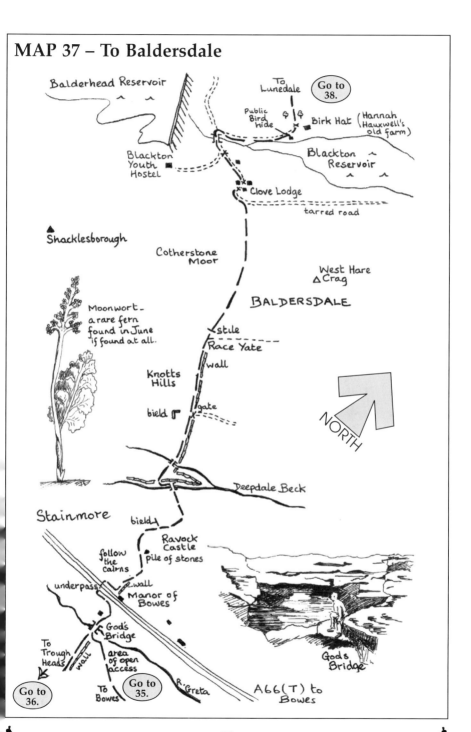

Balderhead Reservoir

To Lunedale

Go to 38.

Public Bird hide

Birk Hat (Hannah Hauxwell's old farm)

Blackton Youth Hostel

Blackton Reservoir

Clove Lodge

tarred road

▲ Shacklesborough

Cotherstone Moor

West Hare △Crag

BALDERSDALE

Moonwort – a rare fern found in June if found at all.

stile

Race Yate

wall

Knotts Hills

bield

gate

NORTH

Deepdale Beck

Stainmore

bield

Ravock Castle

follow the cairns

pile of stones

underpass

wall

Manor of Bowes

God's Bridge

To Trough Heads

wall

area of open access

God's Bridge

Go to 36.

To Bowes

Go to 35.

R. Greta

A66(T) to Bowes

MAP 38 – To Lunedale

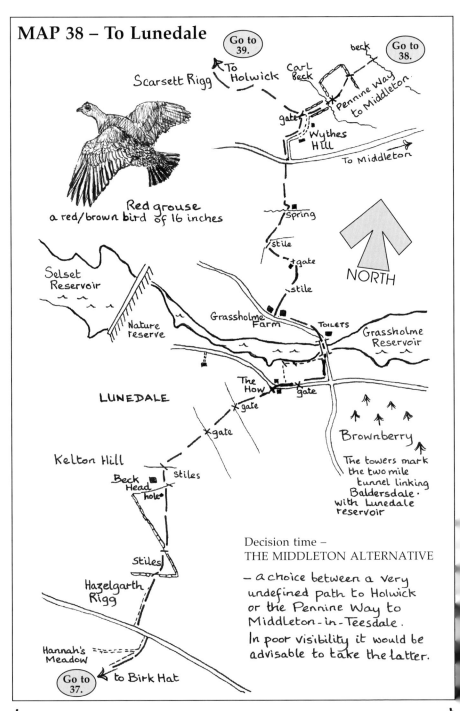

Go to 39.

Go to 38.

Scarsett Rigg

To Holwick

Carl Beck

beck

Pennine Way to Middleton

gate

Wythes Hill

To Middleton

Red grouse
a red/brown bird of 16 inches

spring

stile

gate

NORTH

stile

Selset Reservoir

Nature reserve

Grassholme Farm

TOILETS

Grassholme Reservoir

LUNEDALE

The How

gate

gate

gate

Brownberry

Kelton Hill

Stiles

Beck Head

hole

The towers mark the two mile tunnel linking Baldersdale with Lunedale reservoir

Stiles

Hazelgarth Rigg

Decision time –
THE MIDDLETON ALTERNATIVE

– a choice between a very undefined path to Holwick or the Pennine Way to Middleton-in-Teesdale.
In poor visibility it would be advisable to take the latter.

Hannah's Meadow

Go to 37.

to Birk Hat

MAP 39 – To Holwick

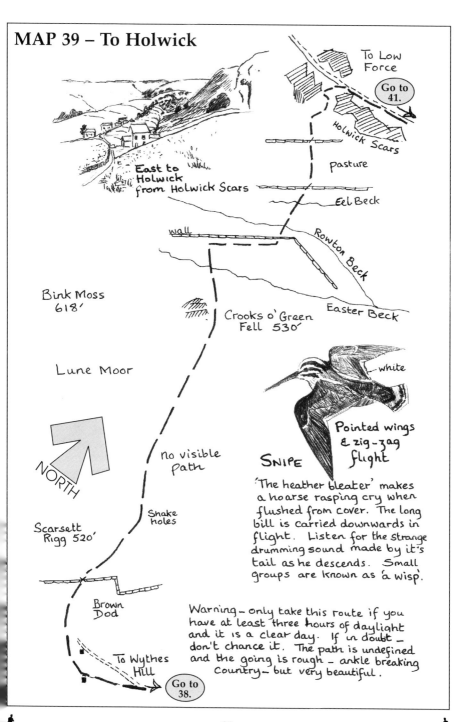

To Low Force

Go to 41.

Holwick Scars

East to Holwick from Holwick Scars

Pasture

Eel Beck

Wall

Rowton Beck

Bink Moss 618'

Crooks o' Green Fell 530'

Easter Beck

Lune Moor

white

NORTH

no visible path

SNIPE

Pointed wings & zig-zag flight

'The heather bleater' makes a hoarse rasping cry when flushed from cover. The long bill is carried downwards in flight. Listen for the strange drumming sound made by it's tail as he descends. Small groups are known as 'a wisp'.

Shake holes

Scarsett Rigg 520'

Brown Dod

To Wythes Hill

Go to 38.

Warning – only take this route if you have at least three hours of daylight and it is a clear day. If in doubt – don't chance it. The path is undefined and the going is rough – ankle breaking country – but very beautiful.

MAP 40 – *The Middleton Alternative*

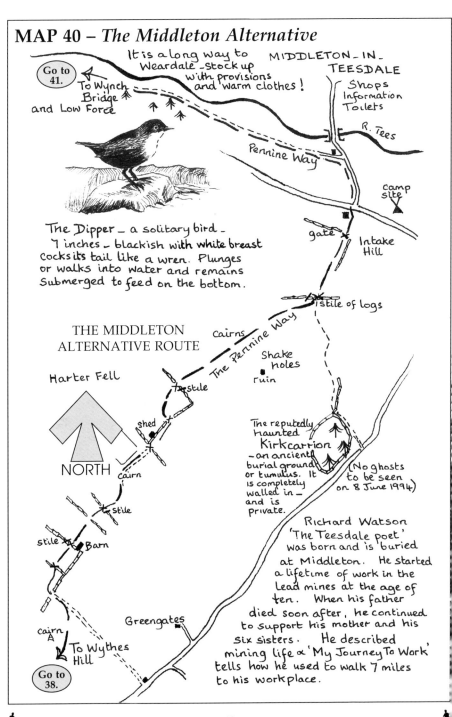

Go to 41.

It is a long way to Weardale - stock up with provisions and warm clothes!

MIDDLETON - IN - TEESDALE

To Wynch Bridge and Low Force

Shops
Information
Toilets

R. Tees

Pennine Way

Camp site

The Dipper – a solitary bird –
7 inches – blackish with white breast
Cocks its tail like a wren. Plunges
or walks into water and remains
Submerged to feed on the bottom.

gate

Intake Hill

stile of logs

THE MIDDLETON
ALTERNATIVE ROUTE

Cairns

The Pennine Way

Shake holes

ruin

Harter Fell

stile

shed

The reputedly
haunted
Kirkcarrion
– an ancient
burial ground
or tumulus. It
is completely
walled in –
and is
private.

(No ghosts
to be seen
on 8 June 1994)

NORTH

cairn

stile

stile   Barn

Richard Watson
'The Teesdale poet'
was born and is buried
at Middleton. He started
a lifetime of work in the
lead mines at the age of
ten. When his father
died soon after, he continued
to support his mother and his
six sisters. He described
mining life a 'My Journey To Work'
tells how he used to walk 7 miles
to his workplace.

cairn

To Wythes Hill

Greengates

Go to 38.

MAP 41 – To Cronkley

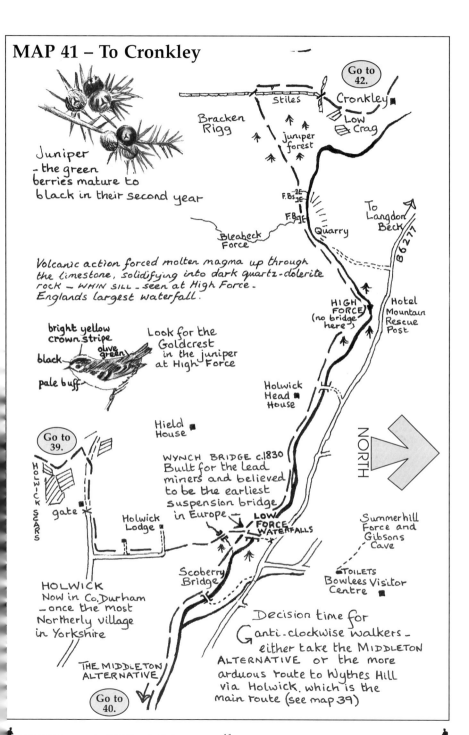

Go to 42.

Cronkley ■

Stiles

Bracken Rigg

Low Crag

juniper forest

Juniper - the green berries mature to black in their second year

F.Bs JE JE

F.B JE

Bleabeck Force

Quarry

To Langdon Beck

B6277

Volcanic action forced molten magma up through the limestone, solidifying into dark quartz-dolerite rock – WHIN SILL - seen at High Force. Englands largest waterfall.

HIGH FORCE (no bridge here)

Hotel Mountain Rescue Post

bright yellow crown stripe

black

olive green

pale buff

Look for the Goldcrest in the juniper at High Force

Holwick Head House

Hield House

Go to 39.

WYNCH BRIDGE c.1830 Built for the lead miners and believed to be the earliest suspension bridge in Europe

HOLWICK SCARS

gate

Holwick Lodge ■

LOW FORCE WATERFALLS

Summerhill Force and Gibsons Cave

NORTH

Scoberry Bridge

■ TOILETS Bowlees Visitor Centre ■

HOLWICK Now in Co.Durham - once the most Northerly village in Yorkshire

Decision time for anti-clockwise walkers - *either take the* MIDDLETON ALTERNATIVE *or the more arduous route to Wythes Hill via Holwick, which is the main route (see map 39)*

THE MIDDLETON ALTERNATIVE

Go to 40.

MAP 42 – To Cow Green Reservoir

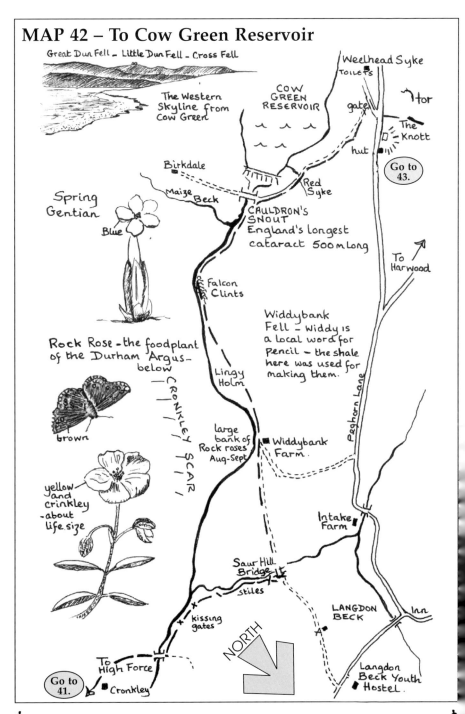

Great Dun Fell – Little Dun Fell – Cross Fell

The Western Skyline from Cow Green

COW GREEN RESERVOIR

Weelhead Syke
Toilets

tor

gate

The Knott

hut

Go to 43.

Birkdale

Maize Beck

Red Syke

CAULDRON'S SNOUT
England's longest cataract 500m long

To Harwood

Spring Gentian

Blue

Falcon Clints

Widdybank Fell – Widdy is a local word for pencil – the shale here was used for making them.

Rock Rose – the foodplant of the Durham Argus – below

brown

CRONKLEY SCAR

Lingy Holm

large bank of Rock roses Aug-Sept

Widdybank Farm.

Peghorn Lane

yellow and crinkley – about life.size

Intake Farm

Saur Hill Bridge

stiles

LANGDON BECK

Inn

kissing gates

NORTH

To High Force

Go to 41.

Cronkley

Langdon Beck Youth Hostel.

MAP 43 – To Harwood

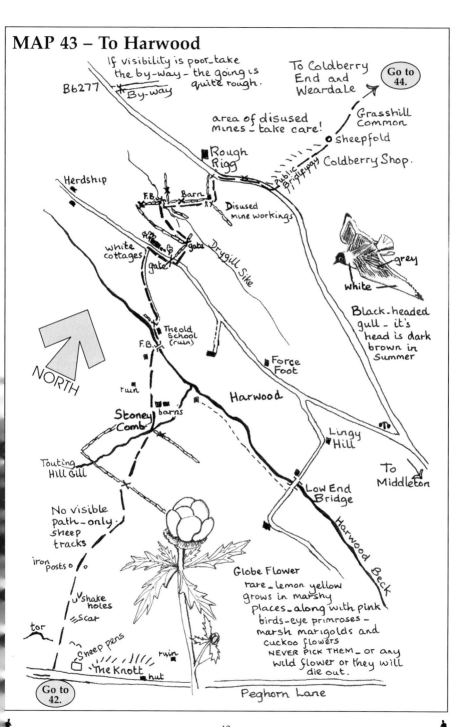

If visibility is poor_take the by-way_the going is quite rough.

B6277 By-way

To Coldberry End and Weardale

Go to 44.

area of disused mines _ take care!

Grasshill Common

sheepfold

Coldberry Shop.

Public Bridleway

Rough Rigg

Herdship

F.B. Barn

Disused mine workings

white cottages

gate gate

gate

Drygill Sike

grey

white

Black-headed gull _ it's head is dark brown in Summer

The old School (ruin)

F.B.

ruin

Force Foot

Harwood

Stoney Comb

barns

Lingy Hill

To Middleton

Touting Hill Gill

Low End Bridge

Harwood Beck

No visible path _ only sheep tracks

iron posts o /o

NORTH

shake holes

Scar

tor

Sheep pens

ruin

The Knott

hut

Globe Flower
rare _ lemon yellow grows in marshy places _ along with pink birds-eye primroses _ marsh marigolds and cuckoo flowers
NEVER PICK THEM _ or any wild flower or they will die out.

Go to 42.

Peghorn Lane

43

MAP 44 – To Burnhope Reservoir

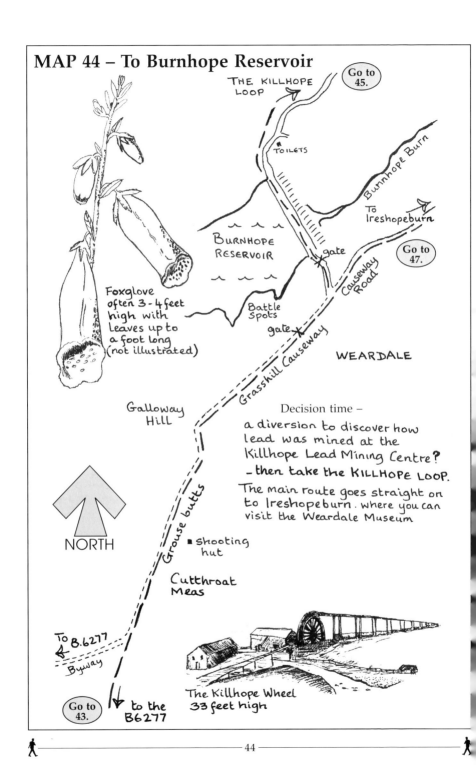

Go to 45.

THE KILLHOPE LOOP

TOILETS

Burnhope Burn

To Ireshopeburn

BURNHOPE RESERVOIR

gate

Go to 47.

Causeway Road

Foxglove often 3-4 feet high with leaves up to a foot long (not illustrated)

Battle Spots

gate

Grasshill Causeway

WEARDALE

Galloway Hill

Decision time –

a diversion to discover how lead was mined at the Killhope Lead Mining Centre?
— then take the KILLHOPE LOOP.

The main route goes straight on to Ireshopeburn. where you can visit the Weardale Museum

Grouse butts

NORTH

■ Shooting hut

Cutthroat Meas

To B.6277

Byway

Go to 43.

↓ to the B6277

The Killhope Wheel 33 feet high

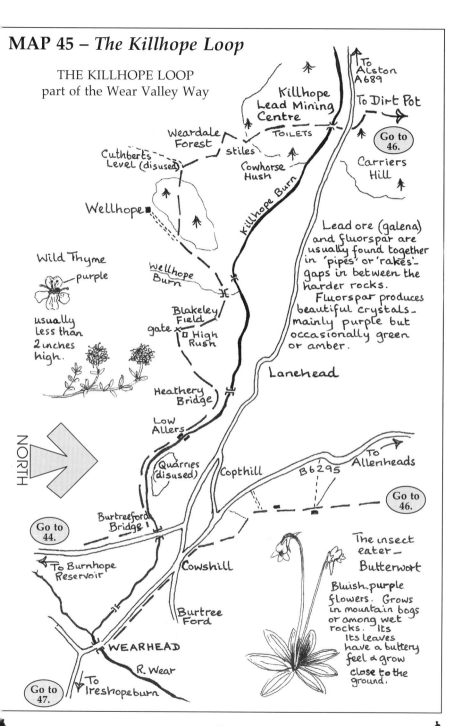

MAP 45 – *The Killhope Loop*

THE KILLHOPE LOOP
part of the Wear Valley Way

To Alston A689

To Dirt Pot

Killhope Lead Mining Centre

TOILETS

Go to 46.

Weardale Forest

Cuthberts Level (disused)

stiles

Cowhorse Hush

Carriers Hill

Wellhope

Killhope Burn

Wild Thyme
purple

usually less than 2 inches high.

Wellhope Burn

Blakeley Field

gate
High Rush

Lead ore (galena) and fluorspar are usually found together in 'pipes' or 'rakes'- gaps in between the harder rocks.
    Fluorspar produces beautiful crystals- mainly purple but occasionally green or amber.

Lanehead

Heathery Bridge

Low Allers

NORTH

Quarries (disused)

Copthill

To Allenheads

B6295

Go to 46.

Go to 44.

Burtreeford Bridge

To Burnhope Reservoir

Cowshill

Burtree Ford

WEARHEAD

R. Wear

Go to 47.

To Ireshopeburn

The insect eater – Butterwort

Bluish.purple flowers. Grows in mountain bogs or among wet rocks. Its Its leaves have a buttery feel & grow close to the ground.

45

MAP 46 – *The Killhope Loop*

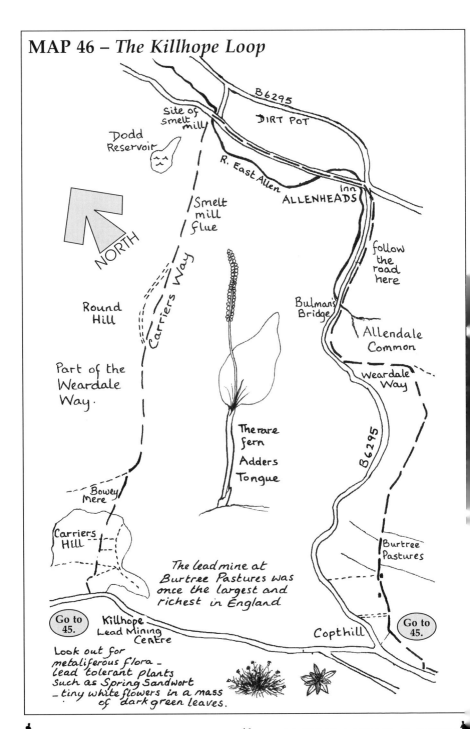

B6295

DIRT POT

Site of smelt mill

Dodd Reservoir

R. East Allen

ALLENHEADS

Inn

NORTH

Smelt mill flue

Carriers Way

follow the road here

Round Hill

Bulmans Bridge

Allendale Common

Weardale Way

Part of the Weardale Way.

B6295

The rare fern

Adders Tongue

Bowey Mere

Carriers Hill

Burtree Pastures

The lead mine at Burtree Pastures was once the largest and richest in England

Go to 45.

Killhope Lead Mining Centre

Copthill

Go to 45.

Look out for metaliferous flora – lead tolerant plants such as Spring Sandwort – tiny white flowers in a mass of dark green leaves.

MAP 47 – To Westgate

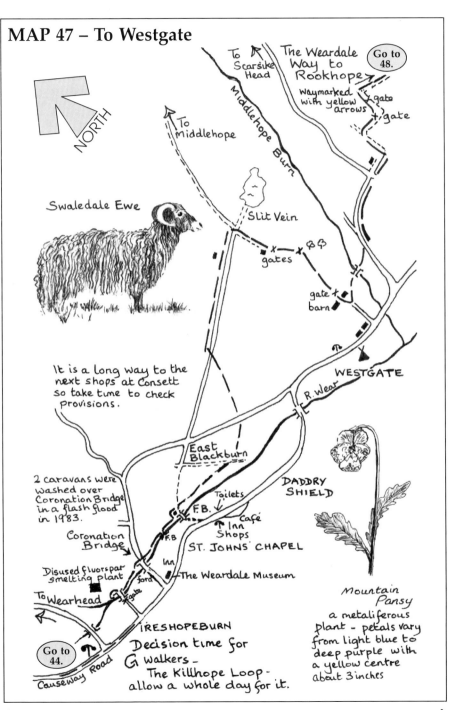

NORTH

To Scarsike Head

The Weardale Way to Rookhope

Go to 48.

Waymarked with yellow arrows

gate

gate

To Middlehope

Middlehope Burn

Swaledale Ewe

Slit Vein

gates

gate

gate
barn

It is a long way to the next shops at Consett so take time to check provisions.

WESTGATE

R. Wear

East Blackburn

DADDRY SHIELD

2 caravans were washed over Coronation Bridge in a flash flood in 1983.

Toilets

F.B.

Café
Inn
Shops

ST. JOHNS CHAPEL

Coronation Bridge

F.B

Inn

Disused fluorspar smelting plant

Ford

The Weardale Museum

To Wearhead

gate

Go to 44.

Causeway Road

IRESHOPEBURN

Decision time for G walkers –

The Killhope Loop – allow a whole day for it.

Mountain Pansy

a metaliferous plant – petals vary from light blue to deep purple with a yellow centre about 3 inches

MAP 48 – To Rookhope

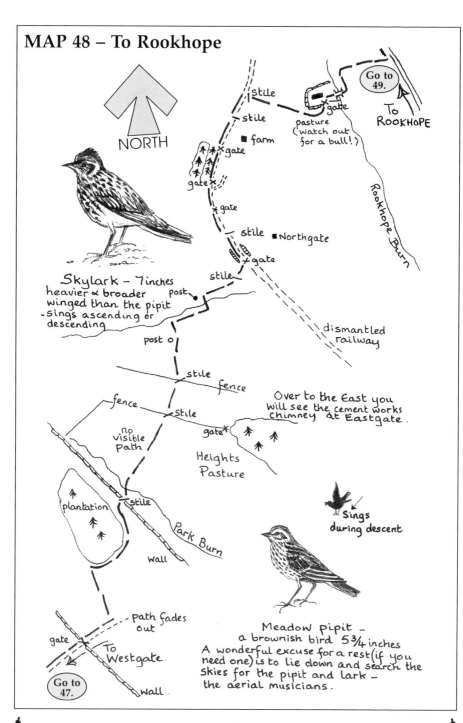

NORTH

stile

stile

farm

Go to 49.

To ROOKHOPE

pasture (watch out for a bull!)

gate

gate

gate

stile ■ Northgate

gate

stile

Rookhope Burn

post

Skylark – 7 inches
heavier & broader
winged than the pipit
-sings ascending or
descending

post o

dismantled railway

stile fence

fence

stile

no visible Path

gate

Over to the East you
will see the cement works
chimney at Eastgate.

Heights Pasture

plantation

stile

Park Burn

wall

Sings during descent

path fades out

gate

To Westgate.

Go to 47.

wall

Meadow pipit –
a brownish bird 5¾ inches
A wonderful excuse for a rest (if you
need one) is to lie down and search the
skies for the pipit and lark –
the aerial musicians.

MAP 49 – To Park Head Quarry

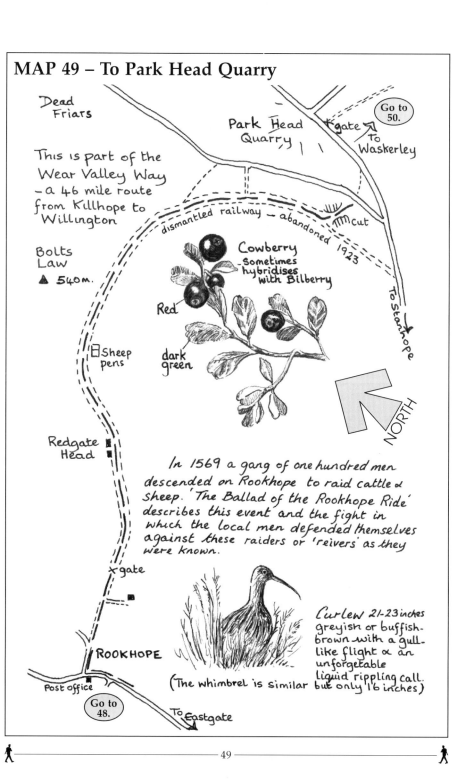

Dead Friars

Park Head Quarry

Go to 50.

gate
To Waskerley

This is part of the Wear Valley Way – a 46 mile route from Killhope to Willington

dismantled railway – abandoned 1923

cut

Bolts Law
▲ 540m.

Cowberry - sometimes hybridises with Bilberry

Red

dark green

To Stanhope

Sheep pens

NORTH

Redgate Head

In 1569 a gang of one hundred men descended on Rookhope to raid cattle & sheep. 'The Ballad of the Rookhope Ride' describes this event and the fight in which the local men defended themselves against these raiders or 'reivers' as they were known.

gate

ROOKHOPE

Curlew 21-23 inches greyish or buffish-brown with a gull-like flight & an unforgetable liquid rippling call.

Post office

(The whimbrel is similar but only 16 inches)

Go to 48.

To Eastgate

MAP 50 – To Waskerley

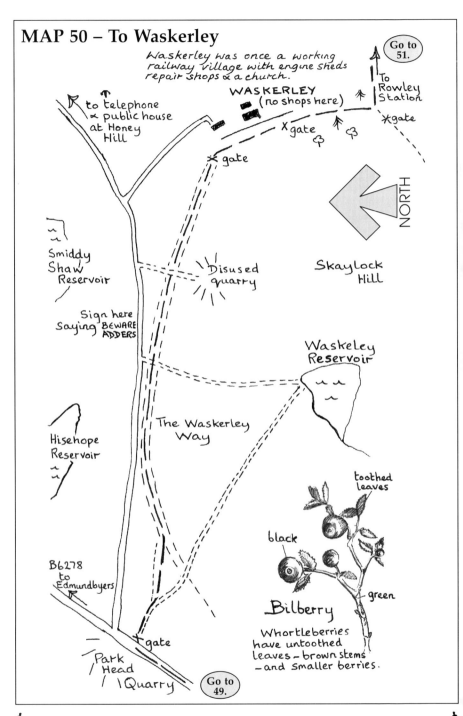

Waskerley was once a working railway village with engine sheds repair shops & a church.

WASKERLEY
(no shops here)

Go to 51.

To Rowley Station

✗gate

↖ to telephone & public house at Honey Hill

✗ gate

✗ gate

NORTH

Smiddy Shaw Reservoir

Disused quarry

Skaylock Hill

Sign here Saying BEWARE ADDERS

Waskeley Reservoir

Hisehope Reservoir

The Waskerley Way

toothed leaves

black

green

Bilberry

B6278 to Edmundbyers

gate

Whortleberries have untoothed leaves – brown stems – and smaller berries.

Park Head Quarry

Go to 49.

MAP 51 – To Rowley Station

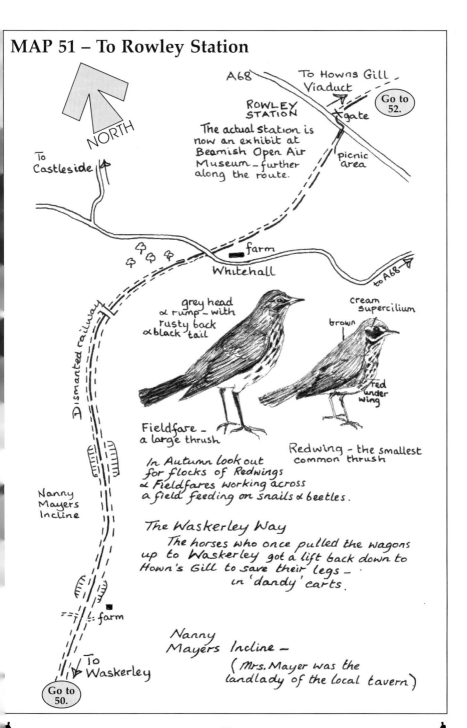

NORTH

To Castleside

A68

To Howns Gill Viaduct

Go to 52.

ROWLEY STATION

The actual station is now an exhibit at Beamish Open Air Museum – further along the route.

gate

picnic area

to A68

farm
Whitehall

Dismantled railway

grey head & rump - with rusty back & black tail

Fieldfare - a large thrush

cream supercilium

brown

red under wing

Redwing - the smallest common thrush

In Autumn look out for flocks of Redwings & Fieldfares working across a field feeding on snails & beetles.

Nanny Mayers Incline

The Waskerley Way
The horses who once pulled the wagons up to Waskerley got a lift back down to Hown's Gill to save their legs -
in 'dandy' carts.

Nanny Mayers Incline -
(Mrs. Mayer was the landlady of the local tavern)

farm

To Waskerley

Go to 50.

MAP 52 – To Consett

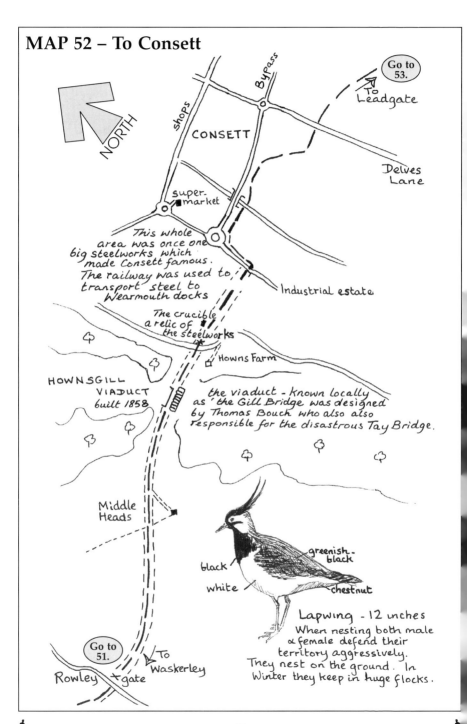

NORTH

Bypass

Go to 53.

To Leadgate

shops

CONSETT

Delves Lane

super-market

This whole area was once one big steelworks which made Consett famous. The railway was used to transport steel to Wearmouth docks

Industrial estate

The crucible a relic of the steelworks

Howns Farm

HOWNSGILL VIADUCT built 1858

the viaduct - Known locally as 'the Gill Bridge was designed by Thomas Bouch who also also responsible for the disastrous Tay Bridge.

Middle Heads

greenish-black

black

white

chestnut

Lapwing - 12 inches

When nesting both male & female defend their territory aggressively. They nest on the ground. In Winter they keep in huge flocks.

Go to 51.

To Waskerley

Rowley gate

MAP 53 – Leadgate

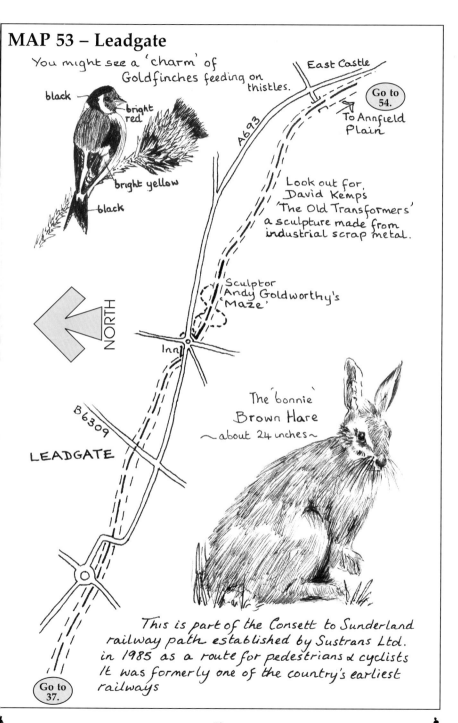

You might see a 'charm' of Goldfinches feeding on thistles.

black

bright red

bright yellow

black

East Castle

A693

Go to 54.

To Annfield Plain

Look out for David Kemp's 'The Old Transformers' a sculpture made from industrial scrap metal.

Sculptor Andy Goldworthy's 'Maze'

NORTH

Inn

B6309

LEADGATE

The 'bonnie' Brown Hare ~ about 24 inches ~

Go to 37.

This is part of the Consett to Sunderland railway path established by Sustrans Ltd. in 1985 as a route for pedestrians & cyclists It was formerly one of the country's earliest railways

MAP 54 – To Stanley

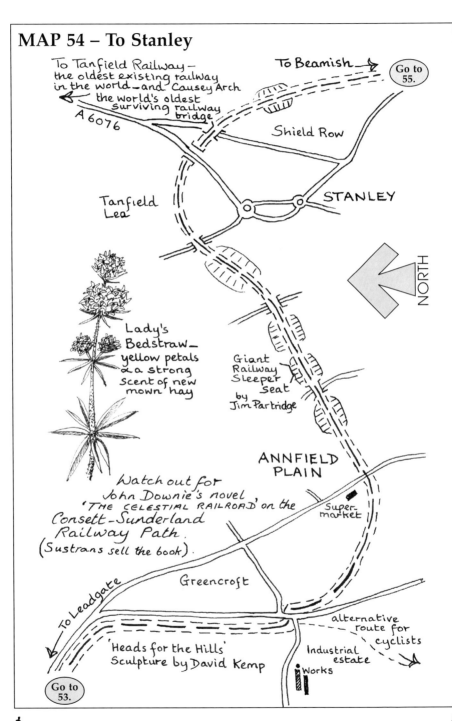

To Tanfield Railway – the oldest existing railway in the world – and Causey Arch the world's oldest surviving railway bridge

To Beamish

Go to 55.

A 6076

Shield Row

Tanfield Lea

STANLEY

NORTH

Lady's Bedstraw – yellow petals & a strong scent of new mown hay

Giant Railway Sleeper Seat by Jim Partridge

ANNFIELD PLAIN

Watch out for John Downie's novel 'THE CELESTIAL RAILROAD' on the Consett-Sunderland Railway Path. (Sustrans sell the book).

Super-market

To Leadgate

Greencroft

alternative route for cyclists

'Heads for the Hills' Sculpture by David Kemp

Industrial estate

Works

Go to 53.

MAP 55 – To Chester-le-Street

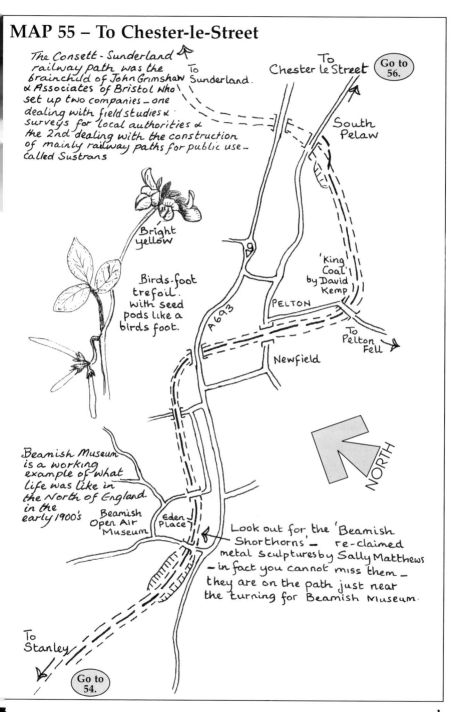

The Consett-Sunderland railway path was the brainchild of John Grimshaw & Associates of Bristol who set up two companies — one dealing with field studies & surveys for local authorities & the 2nd dealing with the construction of mainly railway paths for public use — called Sustrans

To Sunderland.

To Chester le Street

Go to 56.

South Pelaw

Bright yellow

Birds-foot trefoil. with seed pods like a birds foot.

'King Coal' by David Kemp

A693

PELTON

To Pelton Fell

Newfield

NORTH

Beamish Museum is a working example of what life was like in the North of England in the early 1900's

Beamish Open Air Museum

Eden Place

Look out for the 'Beamish Shorthorns' — re-claimed metal sculptures by Sally Matthews — in fact you cannot miss them — they are on the path just near the turning for Beamish Museum.

To Stanley

Go to 54.

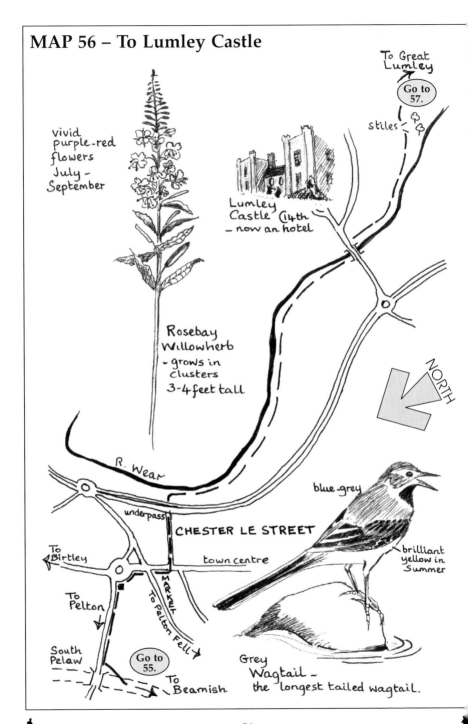

MAP 56 – To Lumley Castle

To Great Lumley

Go to 57.

stiles

vivid purple-red flowers July – September

Lumley Castle (14th – now an hotel

Rosebay Willowherb – grows in clusters 3-4 feet tall

NORTH

R. Wear

blue-grey

underpass

CHESTER LE STREET

To Birtley

town centre

brilliant yellow in Summer

To Pelton

Market To Pelton Fell

South Pelaw

Go to 55.

To Beamish

Grey Wagtail – the longest tailed wagtail.

MAP 57 – To Finchale Abbey

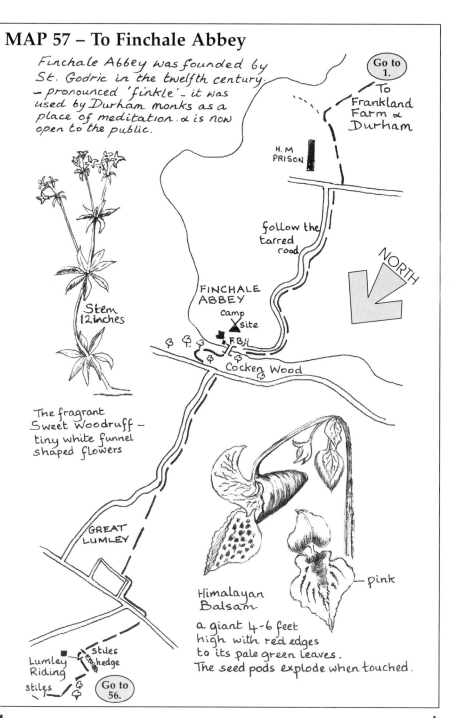

Finchale Abbey was founded by St. Godric in the twelfth century. - pronounced 'finkle' - it was used by Durham monks as a place of meditation. & is now open to the public.

Go to 1.

To Frankland Farm & Durham

H. M PRISON

follow the tarred road

NORTH

FINCHALE ABBEY

camp site

F.B.

Cocken Wood

Stem 12 inches

The fragrant Sweet Woodruff – tiny white funnel shaped flowers

GREAT LUMLEY

Himalayan Balsam

pink

a giant 4-6 feet high with red edges to its pale green leaves. The seed pods explode when touched.

stiles hedge

Lumley Riding

stiles

Go to 56.

Index to Route Maps and approximate mileage

Map numbers are identical to page numbers in this book.

N.B. To convert miles into kilometres, multiply by 8 and divide the result by 5.

Index to Illustrations
— of Flora & Fauna seen while researching the route —
Flora

Butterflies & other insects

Fauna

Birds

N.B. Measurements quoted in this book indicate length of bird from tip of bill – to tip of tail.

Comparative Bird Sizes – the average size of some common birds to help with identification.

Average length from tip of bill to tip of tail:

Crow	18 inches	Pigeon	16 inches
Blackbird	10 inches	Starling	8 inches
Robin	$5^1/_2$ inches	Wren	$3^3/_4$ inches

Index to Illustrations Continued

Also illustrated:

Author's note —

I have included only flora and fauna seen on the route of the **Durham Round** during the exploratory walks between 1991 and 1994. Two exceptions are Adder's tongue and the rare Moonwort which I did not see, but inlcuded in the hope that future walkers might be more fortunate. The illustrations give only a rough indication of what you might see and walkers are advised to take with them comprehensive field books of their main interests.

SAFETY AND SURVIVAL

If you plan to walk the **Durham Round** you are advised to send away for the following free information leaflet —

Safety on the Durham Fells from the Countryside Dept., Durham County Council, County Hall, Durham DH1 5UQ.

Wind chill factor —

Remember a 20 m.p.h. wind at a temperature of 10°F is equivalent to a temperature of **Minus 25°F**. Strong winds, frequently winds over 40 m.p.h. can blow in any season. Night frosts are not uncommon even in summer.

Hypothermia – Exhaustion – Exposure

Hypothermia occurs when your core (heart, lungs, etc.) temperature drops to below 35°C (95°F). If your core temperature drops to these levels then your **Vital Organs** cease to function. It can take as little as one hour from first symptoms to **Death.**

Symptoms:–
uncontrollable shivering, abnormal vision, irrational or violent behaviour, pallor, slurred speech, confusion, stumbling followed by collapse and unconsciousness.

Treatment:–
Warm up immediately
Find or improvise shelter
Conserve energy – exercise is energy sapping
Raise blood sugar level with hot sugary drinks
Get into dry clothes and into a sleeping bag –
Then pull up a survival bag around you
Or wrap up in a space blanket.

If the patient is in a bad way then someone else should get in beside him/her while someone goes for help. Remember that if one member of the group is suffering from exhaustion/exposure then others may be suffering also.

Important:–
the patient should not be rubbed or given alcohol. Alcohol may cause a sudden rush of cold blood from outer areas to the heart **which could be fatal.** A hot water bottle against the skin could have the same effect. It is best to treat hypothermia really seriously and **send for help. Remember Cold plus Wet = Dead!**

International Distress Signal:–
   3 Blasts on a whistle   –   Plus repeats
or 3 Flashes on a torch   –   Plus repeats
People sent for help should carry the exact location-grid reference.

YOUR FEET

Blisters:–
           As soon as you feel any soreness
               STOP – AT ONCE
and cover with a plaster or moleskin as a preventative against further
friction which will eventually cause a blister.

The 'golden rule' once you have a blister, is to remove the cause and
to avoid popping it. On a walk this is impractical – if you do not pop
it and have to continue walking it will pop itself and probably become
infected. If you have left it until a blister has former, pop it with a sterile
needle, cover it with a sterile plaster and change into clean socks.

Prevention
Make sure your boots are well broken in before you start the *Durham
Round*. Avoid nylon socks – next to your skin especially. Wear two pairs
of socks. Cover any known trouble spots with moleskin before you set
off.

Cracked heels – Can be very painful.
Wash and dry your feet carefully and apply vaseline or lanolin cream.
If a crack starts to bleed apply antiseptic and cover with a sterile plaster.

Athlete's Foot
A fungus condition found usually between the toes and on the soles of
the feet, where the skin flakes and peels. Anti-fungal foot powders or
gels must be used daily and socks changed regularly, (avoid nylon
socks) after a thorough washing and drying. If you are prone to
athlete's foot it may be advisable to take sandals with you for
changing into after the days walk.

Look where you put your feet
Look out for man-made hazards as well as natural ones such as rabbit
holes. Mine shafts, shake holes, wells, barbed wire and farm machinery
are often hidden, overgrown with grass. It is safest to keep to a well

trodden path, but even on these, you are advised to stop walking if you want to look at the view. To avoid hazards you must look where you are putting your feet at all times. A sprained ankle will mean the end of your walk.

Snakes

Adders will attack only if they are surprised. If one hears you coming it will normally make off as fast as it can – which is not very fast. Springtime is the most common time for adders – they dislike heat so in summer you are more likely to see them in the cool of the early morning.

Lightning

Avoid walking or standing upright on exposed ridges or on top of a hill – there will be nothing higher for the lightning to hit first.

In bad weather conditions – play safe. True veterans know when to admit defeat. Play on the safe side and you too will live to be a veteran! Every walker must be aware that the human body is susceptible to hypothermia in cold, wet weather and that near starving conditions can be avoided by careful planning. Emergency supplies such as chocolate, mint cake, dried fruit or fruit cake should always be carried with you. You should take a bivvy bag with you and a space blanket – just in case the unexpected happens.

If you intend to camp prepare yourself by reading Kevin Walker's excellent book 'Wild Country Camping' published by Constable 1989. Also 'The Long Distance Walkers Handbook' by Barbara Blatchford published by A. & C. Black 1986. Addresses of Tourist Information Centres appear on page 69. Sending for their free literature will help you plan your walk in advance.

COMFORT AND EASE OF TRAVELLING

In any one day a walker can encounter extremes in weather conditions and freezing temperatures – hot sunshine – snow, sleet and hail – torrential rain. Walkers have to be prepared for continually changing their clothing in order to stay comfortable.

You will need a light rucksack to carry –
1. a lightweight waterproof and trousers
2. Spare sweaters and socks
3. a woollen hat and gloves (even in summer)
4. survival bag, space blanket, first aid pack.
5. plasters, moleskins and small folding scissors
6. whistle, torch and penknife
7. emergency rations (chocolate, dried fruit, etc.)
8. your food and drink for the day

About your clothing – ask yourself
Is it comfortable?
Is it durable?
Does it do the job intended?

You should be able to answer yes to all these questions – and you should have pocket room to stow your **Durham Round** book and the relevant O.S. maps. Don't forget your compass!

Recommended reading:
The Expedition Guide by Wally Keay
A Compendium of information on safe adventure.
Price £12.95 from The Duke of Edinburgh's Award Scheme,
Unit 18/19 Stewartfield Industrial Estate, Edinburgh EH6 5RQ.

SUGGESTED PLACES TO STAY
Bed & Breakfast, Camp Sites and Youth Hostels

Barnard Castle area
West Roods Farm, Boldron,
Barnard Castle
DL12 9SW
Tel: (01833) 690116

Baldersdale Youth Hostel,
Blackton, Baldersdale,
Barnard Castle,
Co. Durham.
Tel: (01833) 650629

Beamish
Bobby Shafto Caravan Park
& Camp Site,
Canberry Plantation,
Beamish,
Co.Durham.
Tel: (0191) 370 1776

Bowes
Mrs. T. Milner,
East Mellwaters Farm,
Bowes, Nr. Barnard Castle.
Tel: (01833) 628269

Castleside area
Manor Park & Camp Site,
Allensford,
Castleside,
Co. Durham
DH8 9HD.
Tel: (01207) 503706

Chester-le-Street area
High Flatts Farm,
Chester-le-Street,
Co. Durham
DH2 1BL
Tel: (0191) 388 3371

Consett Y.M.C.A.
Parliament Street,
Consett,
Co. Durham
DH8 5DH.
Tel: (01207) 502680/501852

Darlington
The Arts Centre,
Vane Terrace,
Darlington
DL3 7AX.
Tel: (01325) 483271

Durham area
Durham Youth Hostel,
Providence Row,
Durham City
Tel: Y.H.A. (0191) 221 2101

University of Durham,
Old Shire Hall,
Durham City.
Tel: (0191) 374 3454

Finchale Abbey Caravan Park,
Finchale Abbey (5 miles north)
Durham.
Tel: (0191) 386 6528

Edmundbyers
Edmundbyers Youth Hostel,
Low House,
Edmundbyers,
Co. Durham
DH8 9NL
Tel: (01207) 255651

Hartlepool area
Crimdon Dene Caravan Park,
Blackhall Rocks,
Co. Durham
TS27 4BN.
Tel: (01429) 267801

Dene Mouth Caravan Park,
Coast Road,
Blackhall Rocks,
TS27 4BL.
Tel: (0191) 586 0963

Holwick
Y.H.A. Camping Barn,
Grid Ref. NY 914270
To book Tel: (01833) 622372

Ireshopeburn
Weardale House,
Ireshopeburn.
Contact:
Y.M.C.A. Residential Office,
Herrington Burn,
Houghton-le-Spring,
Co. Durham
DH4 4JW.
Tel: (0191) 385 2822

Langdon Beck
Langdon Beck Youth Hostel,
Forest in Teedale,
Co. Durham,
DL12 0XN.
Tel: (01833) 622228

Middleton-in-Teesdale
Daleview Caravan Park,
Middleton-in-Teesdale,
Co. Durham
DL12 0TR.
Tel: (01833) 640233

Wythes Hill Farm
Lunedale, Middleton.
Tel: (01833) 640349

Hudeway Outdoor Centre
Hudeway Farm East,
Stacks Lane,
Middleton-in-Teesdale,
Co. Durham.
Tel: (01833) 640012

Piercebridge
Mrs. A. Graham,
Holme House,
Piercebridge,
Darlington.
Tel: (01325) 374280

Seaham
Harbour View Hotel,
18 North Terrace *(on the sea front)*,
Seaham,
Co. Durham.
Tel: (0191) 581 4386

Stanley/Annfield Plain area
Harperley Caravan Park,
Harperley,
Near Stanley,
Co. Durham.
Tel: (01207) 234168

Wearhead
Grid Ref. Ny 851 387
Y.H.A. Camping Barn
To book: Tel: (01833) 622372

Winston
Winston Caravan Park,
The Old Forge,
Winston,
Co. Durham.
Tel: (01325) 730228

The above are guest houses providing bed & breakfast, youth hostels and camp sites taking tents along the **Durham Round** route. It is not comprehensive.

For a more complete list send for Durham County Council's 'Holiday Guide' and Teesdale District Council's Accommodation Guide — Northumbria Tourist Board, Aykley Heads, Durham DH1 5UX. Tel: (0191) 384 3720.

TOURIST INFORMATION

Details of things to do and see can be obtained from the following Information Centres:—

Sustrans, Rockwood House, Stanley, Co. Durham.

Barnard Castle Information Centre, 43 Galgate, Barnard Castle, Co. Durham DL12 8EL.

Darlington Information Centre, Horsemarket, Darlington, Co. Durham DL1 5QU.

Durham City Information Centre, Market Place, Durham City, Co. Durham DH1 3NJ.

Hartlepool Art Gallery Information Centre, Church Square, Hartlepool, TS24 7EQ.

Middleton-in-Teesdale Information Centre, Middleton Crafts, The Courtyard of the Teesdale Hotel, Middleton-in-Teesdale, Co. Durham DL12 0QG.

Shotley Bridge Information Centre, 1 Church Bank, Shotley Bridge, Co. Durham DH8 0HF.

Durham Dales Centre, Market Place, Stanhope, Co. Durham DL13 2FJ.

Station House Field Centre, Castle Eden Walkway, Thorpe Thewles, Stockton-on-Tees.

For Bus Routes in Co. Durham contact the Public Transport Group, County Hall, Aykley Heads, Durham City, Co. Durham DH1 5UQ.

Day one

Where:

From.............................to.............................

Time taken   Distance covered

Night time arrangements

Events / People met / Wildlife

Day two

Where:

From.............................to.............................

Time taken   Distance covered

Night time arrangements

Events / People met / Wildlife

Day three

Where:

From.............................to.............................

Time taken   Distance covered

Night time arrangements

Day four

Where:
From..to..

Time taken   Distance covered

Night time arrangements

Events / People met / Wildlife

Day five

Where:
From..to..

Time taken   Distance covered

Night time arrangements

Events / People met / Wildlife

Day six

Where:
From..to..

Time taken   Distance covered

Night time arrangements

Day seven

Where:

From..................................to..

Time taken   Distance covered

Night time arrangements

Events / People met / Wildlife

Day eight

Where:

From...........................to...

Time taken   Distance covered

Night time arrangements

Events / People met / Wildlife

Day nine

Where:

From...........................to...

Time taken   Distance covered

Night time arrangements

Day ten

Where:

From…………………………………to……………………………………

Time taken   Distance covered

Night time arrangements

Events / People met / Wildlife

Day eleven

Where:

From…………………………………to……………………………………

Time taken   Distance covered

Night time arrangements

Events / People met / Wildlife

Day twelve

Where:

From…………………………………to……………………………………

Time taken   Distance covered

Night time arrangements

Day thirteen

Where:

From...to..

Time taken   Distance covered

Night time arrangements

Events / People met / Wildlife

Day fourteen

Where:

From...to..

Time taken   Distance covered

Night time arrangements

Events / People met / Wildlife

Day fifteen

Where:

From...to..

Time taken   Distance covered

Night time arrangements

NORTHUMBERLAND

Derwent Reservoir

YH
Edmundbyers

Allenheads

Killhope

Rookhope

Wearhead

Westgate

Stanhope

River Wear

Cow Green Reservoir

Langdon Beck
Y.H.

Middleton-in-Teesdale

River Tees

Y.H.

Barnard Castle

CUMBRIA

Bowes

River Greta

Gr

Tan Hill

Main Route − − − − −
The five loops ✗ ✗ ✗ ✗
Rivers Tees, Wear & Greta ───────

THE DU

R. Wear

eamish

anley

Chester
le Street

NORTH SEA

Seaham

South
Hetton

Easington
Colliery

urham

Pittington

Horden

Wingate

Blackhall

Station
Town

Crimdon

Hartlepool

URHAM

Stillington

Thorpe
Thewles

Bishopton

iercebridge

TEESSIDE

Sadberge

Darlington

Middleton - one - row

Croft
on Tees

Girsby

R Tees

YORKSHIRE

INDEX TO PLACE NAMES

Index to Place Names Continued